Parents to the End

Parents to the End

- - - - - - - - - - - -

How Baby Boomers Can Parent for
Peace of Mind, Foster Responsibility in Their
Adult Children, and Keep Their
Hard-Earned Money

- - - - - - - - -

LINDA M. HERMAN, LMHC

- - - - -

NTI UPSTREAM
CHICAGO

NTI UPSTREAM
180 N. MICHIGAN AVE., STE. 700
CHICAGO, ILLINOIS 60601

NTI UPSTREAM books may be purchased for educational, business, or sales promotional use. For more information about special discounts for bulk purchases or to book a live event, please contact NTI UPSTREAM Special Sales at 312-423-5669.

Grateful acknowledgement to: JEANNE WEBSTER BLANK, author of *The Death of an Adult Child: A Book for and about Bereaved Parents* (copyright 1998, Baywood Publishing Co., Inc.) for the "Four Phases of Grief," Chapter 2, page 23; and to MALCOM S. KNOWLES, ELWOOD F. HOLTON III and RICHARD A. SWANSON, authors of *The Adult Learner* (copyright 2011, Taylor and Francis) for "the six assumptions about an adult learner," pages 64-68.

LEGAL DISCLAIMERS

This book is for informational and educational purposes only; it should not be intended as a substitute for professional psychological, psychiatric, or psychotherapeutic treatment. This book should not be used to prevent, diagnose or treat any mental health conditions or disorders.

The names of children and families, as well as some of the identifying details of events in the case studies, have been changed.

LIBRARY OF CONGRESS CONTROL NUMBER: 2012938933
ISBN: 978-0-9836396-7-1

COVER PHOTO BY GLEN GYSSLER PHOTOGRAPHY
AUTHOR PHOTO BY JAIME HERRERA, JRB MULTIMEDIA
EDITED BY JEFF LINK
Printed in the United States of America

To Robert, Marcus, and Jim

Don't handicap your children by making their lives easy.

ROBERT A. HEINLEIN

Contents

PART ONE

Baby Boomers as Parents of Adult Children

- - - - - - - - - - - - - -

CHAPTER ONE

Post-Adolescent Parenting

"They want the moon," Anna said to her friend as they boarded a plane bound for Kansas City. Her daughter and son-in-law, a struggling couple in their thirties, had just gone to Macy's and charged a new set of living room furniture—expensive living room furniture—which, by any standard, was no small investment. Having just paid for the couple's medical expenses (four thousand dollars when all was said and done), Anna and her husband Larry were not pleased. What was intended as a gift to help the young couple escape credit card debt had only sunk them deeper into trouble. How could their beloved child, a diligent student whom they had raised in a budget-conscious household, forget the valuable lesson of living within one's means?

If this story sounds familiar, that's because, for many of us, footing the bill for our post-adolescent children is indeed the reality of parenting. If you thought your job was done when your child finished high school or college, landed that first job, or finally signed the lease on his first apartment, it may be time to reevaluate your expectations. Most parents look forward to the day when they no longer feel financially or emotionally responsible for their children. But, for many, that day seems hopelessly far off. There is the fear—not unjustifiable— that they'll be the provider and caretaker for their children forever.

Of course in a way that's true. You will always be your child's parent, and you'll always have a role in his life. Determining that role, however, can be difficult, especially with young adults who are not ready or not choosing to assume responsibility for their lives. If you've been to the parenting section of a bookstore recently or browsed your e-reader for relevant titles, you know there is plenty written about parenting children and adolescents. Yet there is surprisingly little guidance for those whose sons and daughters are twenty-three or twenty-six years old and camped out in their childhood basement. Healthy, respectful parents know that it is not their job to control the lives of their children. What they may not know, however, is how to encourage their adult children's growth during the oft-ignored period of post-adolescence. Rather than focusing on what children need to do in order to change, this book focuses on what you can do, active steps you can take, to avoid becoming your child's permanent hotel and bank account.

Anna and Larry are not at all unique. Their story is like that of many baby boomers, who, for a variety of reasons, are still *actively* parenting (or worrying about how to parent) their adult children. Questions like theirs come up repeatedly in my suburban Seattle office, where I work as a psychotherapist. Parents consistently report that their young adults are making financial choices that make no sense, splurging on expensive dinners or transcontinental vacations, yet comfortably ask for and accept money when their bank accounts run dry. It wasn't that way when Anna and Larry started out, not in their minds anyway. Self-made, they neither expected nor received material help from their parents. They built their lives through hard work, wise choices, and determination.

The view that adult children of this generation are less self-sufficient than their parents— that they are less ambitious, less driven to success—may have some basis in reality, but it ignores an important point. If our adult children are looking to us increasingly for support, if they are relying on us to pay for their new living room furniture and pick up their cell phone bills, that dependency may have as much to do with the signals we are sending as parents as with a lack of work ethic.

Expectations in Boomer and Depression-Era Parents

It is true that many adult children have unrealistically high expectations of their parents. They expect Mom and Dad to foot the bill each time they get an unexpected traffic ticket or have to visit the dentist. This is indeed a problem but so is the fact that many baby boomer parents, though they might not care to admit it, place these same high expectations on themselves.

While there is nothing wrong with expecting achievement, we cannot assume that our values and aspirations will automatically be reflected in our children. Unlike our Depression-era parents—who communicated high expectations even though they lacked opportunities to achieve— we baby boomers tend to strive for our own success, without necessarily demanding its prerequisites in our children. Did Anna follow her parents' example, insisting on her daughter's independence? Or did she do just the opposite: setting lower expectations for her children because her parents had set the bar so high? The answer probably lies somewhere in the middle, and Anna's financial position complicates the calculus. Like Anna, many of us have undeservedly modest expectations of independent behavior for our children, complicated by the fact that we have the financial means to rescue them when life's unexpected bumps—like a $4,000 medical bill—get in the way.

Even though independence is coming later for the current crop of young adults, the expectation that young men would build their lives around their roles as providers has been fairly constant over the years. Not so for women, however. Mothers in the 1940s and 1950s were largely stay-at-home women, while many of their daughters (who ushered in the feminist movement) traded their aprons for business suits, motivated by the promise of professional careers. The daughters of *those* women, however, often want to be the primary caretakers for their children, or they want a professional career that affords them more time at home. It is almost a universal law, in fact, that each generation will differentiate itself from its predecessor, casting off at least some of what the prior generation modeled, while hanging on to those values and traditions that are cherished.

As a generation, we boomers parented in an era of affluence. There was no roadmap to tell us when we had crossed the line from nurturing caregivers to debilitating enablers, nor reason to think that by contributing a down payment on our child's first home we'd be setting them up for lifelong dependency. It is understandable why we thought we should help more: because we *could*. "Isn't that what we're supposed to do?" parents often ask: "We have the money."

Unfortunately, helping more may actually mean helping less. Many of my peers, the frustrated parents of needy adult children, find themselves stumped. They're looking for guidance and reassurance they are doing the "right thing," but unsure where to seek solutions when their children act and behave immaturely. Perhaps most important, they want peace of mind as they transition into this new stage of life, in which their children move progressively toward emancipation. Through two-and-a-half decades of therapeutic work with baby boomers and their children, I've been privileged to watch children grow from grade school to adulthood. What I've discovered is that, despite all the parenting books and experts baby boomers may have consulted, a large percentage remain guilty about their performance as parents and apprehensive about what lies ahead. For many, the advantages they've given their children have not yielded the benefits they expected—neither appreciation nor signs of increased motivation—and they're ready for a new approach.

The Sandwich Generation

To understand how we got here, we need to consider how the Depression-era values of our parents' generation shaped our own parenting practices. Depression-era parents may have known abundance and blessings, but these were generally not in material form. For instance, when my mother was growing up, the potatoes consumed in the household were harvested from the backyard garden. She and her six siblings enjoyed the potatoes' starchy insides, while her father found sustenance in the peelings. My mother's first job meant taking the train sixty miles from Youngstown to Cleveland to clean houses—dutifully washing the floors each week, even as an alumnus of her high school's first National Honor Society. Ever frugal, painstakingly meticulous, she tracked every expense in a notebook I've kept to this day. Like many young men and women of her era, she endured hardship with pride because she believed that "sacrifice" and "making do" were natural to building character.

Such a lifestyle invariably led women like my mother to inspire their children toward the kind of professional success that had been unattainable to members of their generation. One woman I interviewed, Diane, has a story that typifies the era. The owner of a candle shop, Diane is a soft-spoken woman with highlighted chin-length hair, who lost her mother before she was ten years old. Raised by her father and an aunt, she knew at a young age not to ask for anything. Her father was a logger in the Cascade Mountains, a headstrong man who was slow to show affection, and slower still to give her money. When Diane got her first job tending plants at a nursery at age fourteen, it was out of financial necessity, not any natural inclination toward botany. She married at twenty. Her father's contribution to the wedding, a far cry from the expensive dresses found in today's glossy bridal magazines, was twenty pounds of unglamorous home-smoked sausage. Several years later, when he lent her $500 for a car, the loan was worth millions to Diane—a sign of his caring which she had craved for years. Although she would have appreciated more time and attention from her father, Diane says she is thankful for what she was given.

Children born between 1946 and 1964 (the "baby boomers") are sometimes referred to as the sandwich generation. Their expectations and values lie somewhere between that of their Depression-era parents, and their own children for whom the next gadget is a credit card-swipe away. Characteristic of the generation is a high level of self-motivation and ambition, a belief that through hard work, focus, and determination one can achieve success and prosperity.

Certainly, baby boomers and their parents witnessed a sharp rise in the availability of educational opportunities and the accessibility of professional careers. Boomer children were able to attend college in unprecedented numbers. For those familiar with Maslow's hierarchy (in which we chart a path from basic needs such as food, sleep, and employment toward progressively more abstract ones), the new generation of post-WWII adolescents and young adults was the first to evolve past pragmatic concerns toward loftier aspirations of spiritual awakening and self-fulfillment. They were known for staging some of the first-ever mass protests in the United States against war and for shrugging off many of the traditions in which they were raised. As the post-war economy of the US continued its growth, this self-reflective and increasingly self-possessed generation positioned itself to take the reins of America's cultural and economic awakening.

But where did this leave Depression-era values like frugality and selflessness, filial devotion, and pride in a humble day's work? If the lessons baby boomers derived from their own parents represent one side of the sandwich, the other side is characterized by how baby boomers' own experiences as parents departed from the values and instruction of their forebears. Diane wanted for her own daughter what she could not have for herself. But the way she attempted to fulfill this wish was not by withholding her praise and affection as her father had done. Instead, it was by satisfying Lynnette's every wish, in this case a high school trip to Cancun and an expensive wedding catered by the finest local restaurant. Lynnette, now in her thirties, is an account executive, and while she is very content with her own life, she's consistently dissatisfied with her mother. As Diane told me in our interview, "She wants me to be there for her when *she* wants me." When Lynnette doesn't need Diane for financial support, she is cold and uncommunicative, which, for Diane, can be extremely painful.

To Help or Not To Help

But as troubling as the stories of Anna and Diane sound, they pale in comparison to others I've heard. Many parents subsidize their adult children's irresponsible behavior in extraordinary ways: paying the monthly rent for their expensive apartments, funding the weekly grocery bill while their children are spending money on pornography, bailing them out of jail after a night of belligerent binge drinking, hiring lawyers to plea down their child's DUI charges, financing their credit card debt, and the list goes on.

But how much help is enough? And when is it okay to stop? For some parents, there are virtually no boundaries to their giving: through gifts of money, room and board, legal assistance, and other charitable donations, they offer their assistance without hesitation. There is the feeling that helping their children is part of their job; the adolescents will one day mature effortlessly into adulthood. Unfortunately, with too much help from Mom and Dad, that may not be the case. Coming to our children's aid time and again can divide us as parents, and engender resentment on the part of our adult children's siblings, many of whom are self-sufficient. I've seen cases of well-meaning parents who've spent their retirement savings and taken out second mortgages to provide financial assistance to their children, only to find their gifts received without so much as a thank you. In some cases, parents even continue working beyond retirement, not to support their own lifestyles, but the lifestyles of their adult children. One of the goals of this book, the primary goal, in fact, is to save you from making those same mistakes.

If it sounds like I'm placing undo blame on parents, that's not my intention. Bad things do happen to well-meaning children and adolescents, and sometimes these circumstances necessitate greater involvement on the part of parents. It hurts parents to see their children flounder, and they may be tempted to step in and help for a variety of valid reasons, especially when their children have kids themselves. But a word to the wise: the most helpless of adult children are often the most skilled at evoking guilt. To stop the flow of money is to be accused of cutting off love, which, for many adult children, is the greatest crime of all. Resisting requests for money was easier for Depression-era parents: for one thing, their parents did not have the financial resources to provide it, and even if they'd had the means, their children wouldn't have considered asking for help. At that time, the expectation was that children approaching age eighteen had a responsibility to get on with their lives. Whether that meant beginning a job or a marriage, joining the military, or going off to college, young people knew that the end of high school signaled childhood's ending as well.

Today, that is far less true. Not only do baby boomers have more disposable income than their parents did, but their children are generally quite comfortable asking for it. At times it can appear as though saying "no" to our children is unthinkable. Even some of the most rational among us have difficulty setting monetary limits, and present-day realities do not make this any easier: rent is higher, education costs more, and the price of gas creeps steadily upward. But perhaps the most important factor contributing to the growing dependency of this era's adult children is that, for too many parents, tolerating their children's discomfort is intolerable.

How did baby boomers come to embrace the notion that their children deserve immunity from hardship and discomfort? Why do we think that our children will be unable to survive a mean boss, or a cramped apartment, or that first rejection letter in a down economy? "I'm not like that," you might be thinking to yourself. "I let my child live her own life." But is that the message you are communicating to your children or a residue of what your parents said to you? Isn't it more likely you said something like, "You can be anything you want to be. Don't listen to that teacher who gave you a C. What does he know?" What comes with having been so successful as a generation is the presumption among us boomers that, if necessary, we can fix any problem. That includes our children's problems, even when our children are nineteen or twenty-six years old and it is developmentally appropriate for them to be doing this problem-solving on their own. By conveying the belief that all problems can be instantly solved with a little sweep of the hand, that the sky is the limit, we are unwittingly setting ourselves up to be leaned upon and blamed by our children.

When parents do too much for their adult kids, they become enablers who encourage their children to continue with immature or inappropriate behavior. Of course few parents set out with the aim of disempowering their children by consistently coming to their rescue, but sometimes that is the result. To assist in our children's healthy transition into adulthood, we must understand our children's wants, needs, and expectations, as well as their ability and intention to meet them.

Family lives are complex, and multiple factors should contribute to a parent's decisions about the duration and kind of help they should offer a child. The same is true for the development of expectations. They can be grand or minimal, liberating or restraining, but they need to reflect the world of the possible. The important thing is for parents to develop realistic expectations for their children, expectations which encourage growth, responsibility, and independence, while respecting the children's rights to pursue their dreams.

CHAPTER TWO

The Happiness Conundrum

A huge cultural shift has occurred in recent decades. Too many of us have come to expect uninterrupted happiness as a natural state of being. Anything less is unacceptable and signals a serious problem, which must be fixed immediately. In therapy sessions and workshops I lead, one of the first things I always ask parents—regardless of their children's age—is "What is the main thing that you want for your children?" The overwhelming response: "We want our children to be happy."

While this desire is only natural, the tendency to prioritize it above all else reveals a core misunderstanding. Happiness stems from our children's commitment to their passions, from their own careers, relationships, and life circumstances as much as our guidance and instruction. True happiness comes when children acquire the skills to manage their lives independently—to discover their own kind of fulfillment, whether or not that matches the vision we have had in mind.

One way to ensure our children will *not* be happy, of course, is to satisfy their every whim. Some of my most miserable teen and young adult clients are those whose every need has been anticipated and met by their parents. Many of these young people honestly believe—or so they claim—that to be uncomfortable or unhappy is not right, and that someone, i.e., their parents, must correct the mistake. This unapologetically hedonist mindset is not unlike that of a drug addict or compulsive gambler searching for his next score. And just as a quick fix only perpetuates the problems these individuals have, so does constantly satisfying our children's cravings keep them looking in the wrong direction for fulfillment.

Current research supports the viewpoint that finding happiness is not quick and easy. Those whose main goal is to attain immediate feelings of pleasure and gratification, who look for happiness in a new iPhone or expensive purse, tend to be less happy than those who seek a more altruistic conception of meaning and purpose. The latter experience what is called "eudaemonic happiness," a deeper, longer-lasting contentment than what can be achieved through material consumption. Unfortunately, as materialism is becoming progressively more important in the United States—and more closely linked with status—happiness is appearing evermore elusive. From 1938 to 2007, symptoms of depression, paranoia, and psychopathology increased among college students, a finding researchers at San Diego State University suggest is attributable to a rising focus on materialism and status, accompanied by a shrinking emphasis on community and the value of a meaning-driven life.[1]

As a therapist, I routinely see evidence of the damaging effect unchecked spending can have on my clients. Many crave material goods: fabulous shoes, transcontinental vacations, gourmet cheeses and fine meats. The desire adult children have for such luxuries is made all the worse when parents use their wealth as leverage.

I once worked with an eighteen-year-old named Harry. The older of two children, Harry was a highly motivated college freshman, a perfectionist when it came to his schoolwork. Throughout his school career, teachers sang his praises, remarking on his academic diligence and respect for authority. Little did they know that at home Harry was a veritable dictator. The household revolved around seeing to it that Harry was happy. But no matter what his family did to please him, Harry wore the same smug, offended expression. In the rare moments when he was considerate, a request was soon to follow.

As it happened, Harry was quite attractive. With strong, well-defined features and the handsome build of a film star, Harry had no shortage of girls interested in him. A prince at home, he had little reason to suffer the indignities of a part-time job or a dingy, low rent apartment. Commuting to a nearby state university suited him just fine: traveling to and from school was easy, after all, since his parents had just bought him his third car, a brand new Mini Cooper. (The first car they had bought him, a ten year-old Honda Civic, was to Harry an embarrassment. His parents replaced it. Three months into driving the newer car, Harry totaled it.)

It never occurred to his parents to say a firm "no" when Harry requested the expensive automobile. The boy was terminally unhappy; something had to be done. On his birthday, weeks before Harry began his freshman year of college, the brand new Mini Cooper appeared in the driveway. "A new beginning," his parents thought. "Harry is happy and we can finally relax." But of course they were wrong.

Harry had never held a job. He had never done chores at home. None of this changed when he started attending college. During his first semester, his seventy-five year old great-aunt came over to the house almost daily to feed his fish and make his bed. She'd babysat Harry as a toddler while his mother worked, and she felt a special devotion toward him, perhaps because she'd never had any children of her own. After awhile her visits had become such an integral part of the family routine that no one found them odd—who could blame her, after all, for spending some time with Harry to try to make him happy?

Harry's younger sister, Karen, on the other hand, was next to invisible in the household. She made her bed politely and went to school each morning without anyone taking notice. Undoubtedly, Karen had needs and interests of her own, but these were of tertiary interest. All eyes were on Harry. If he was unhappy, then something must be done. Yet despite all the attention from his family (and his rotating list of girlfriends), Harry was still a very miserable young man.

Harry's father was no fool. Whenever he reviewed the monthly bills, he was disturbed to find that he and his wife were paying for their son's car, their son's car insurance, their son's gasoline—even their son's monthly cell phone bill. Though uncomfortable serving as his son's primary benefactor, Harry's father had presumed that the expenses would be returned in Harry's contributions to the household, and, eventually, a practical academic degree that would allow his son to support himself in a satisfying career.

That was not how events unfolded. Returning home from classes, Harry would retreat to his bedroom and spend innumerable hours G-chatting with his girlfriends. The new laptop his parents had hoped would encourage Harry to do his homework was used mostly to update his dating profile. Meanwhile, Harry's mother, who worked part-time to help pay for his tuition and car, was like a modern-day Edith Bunker, hustling about from dawn to dusk without a moment's rest. As I got to know Harry, a picture emerged of a young man who was overindulged: given too little structure while consuming an inordinate amount of the family's money, time, and attention.[2]

Of course it cannot be glossed over that Harry was clinically depressed. He showed his depression through sadness and irritability, low energy and sleep problems, hopelessness, and a loss of appetite. Harry spent many hours by himself in his room, thinking about how unhappy he was. I referred him to his family doctor, who prescribed a course of antidepressants designed to improve his mood. But I knew that Harry's condition would not improve significantly until the biggest obstacle was addressed: the fact that his parents' actions were inhibiting his growth.

A few days before Harry's next scheduled visit, I invited his mother and father into the discussion. Speaking to the family as a group, I recommended that there be much less focus on keeping Harry happy. This might sound strange, but I wanted to place more responsibility on Harry for taking charge of his emotions. His parents were doing their part: staying supportive at home and following through with the physician. My professional view was that Harry would benefit from learning that others could not bring him happiness; he had to find it within himself. And, as well as I could, I conveyed to him that not only was it possible for him to find ways to be less depressed, but that doing the work himself would be a major step in his personal development.

After our conversation, Harry's parents agreed to back off on their cheerleading, and little by little Harry's mood improved. His parents came to understand that by expecting nothing from their son, they unwittingly aided in his alienation from the family. Hostage to Harry's moods, they had conveyed to him a confusing message: he was all-powerful, yet too fragile to be treated like a capable young man. As a result, Harry didn't know who he was. He knew something was not right, but he had no clue how to fix it.

I never saw Harry as connected or as happy with his family as when he complained months later (in a very reasonable way) about having to come up with a way to pay for his cell phone bill. He was smiling—as were his parents, who, for the first time, felt in charge of their household. A year later, Harry seemed to be on a healthy path. His plan was to get a part-time job and move into campus housing. His only complaint was that his sister was not being as respectful of their parents as he felt she should. That was a complaint his parents could live with. But they arrived there only when they made a drastic change and stopped trying to make Harry happy.

What Frames Your Child's Perspective?

While we parents have tremendous influence, there are other important factors that affect our children's life views. Regardless of our parenting approach, our influence on our children will be tempered by their personality and stage of development, as well as environmental factors that may be out of our control. We'll take a look at those now.

1. Temperament

Children each have their own temperaments. Sometimes the child who was a "difficult" baby and toddler becomes a high-maintenance teen. Harry certainly fit that category. His parents wanted him to be happy, and he took advantage of their coddling: throwing tantrums resembling those he threw when he was a child.

Some parents describe their children as "score-keepers," too keenly aware of what their siblings are getting and whether the distribution of goods and services is equitable. All children are guilty of some level of scorekeeping, but in certain children the drive to tally each and every grievance leads to anger and hurt. It is important to remember that your best efforts at parenting will not change your child's personality. You may have a child who always sees you as favoring her brother or sister, even if that is not the reality. Our job is not to convince our child that we are being fair. Instead, our task is to make the best judgment call as to how we give of ourselves and our resources

within the family. If confronted by an angry adult child, we should acknowledge his feelings and say we are sorry that he sees the situation
in that light. Then we should move on.

2. *Environmental Factors*

Environmental factors can and do affect one's perspective. Think once
again of Harry's family. His sister, Karen, was invisible for reasons
that went beyond her personality. Preceded in the family by Harry,
who was two years older, Karen was cast as his supporting actress.
Whether or not he was present, the topic of conversation invariably
came back to Harry—his latest mood at home, his success at school,
the most recent altercation he had had with their father. Karen actually
felt sorry for her brother. She couldn't understand why someone with
so much going for him could be so unhappy.

Karen's role was modeled by her parents: to try everything in her
power to make her brother feel better. She complimented his great
looks and his grades; fixed special treats for him when he returned
home from campus without being asked; took his dirty clothes to the
laundry room. When that wasn't successful, Karen did the only other
thing she knew how to do well: make things easy on her parents by
becoming invisible. That meant doing nothing to make waves. Karen
asked for little, showed appreciation for what she was given, kept her
room clean, and generally tried to be a dutiful daughter. When Harry
launched into tirades against their parents, Karen watched anxiously
from afar until she couldn't take it anymore and had to retreat to her
room. When she heard Harry's bedroom door slam, signaling the end
of the argument, she came out from hiding and tried to comfort her
parents, telling them what good parents they were and supplying
Harry with a long list of excuses.

During that difficult time, Karen had a hard time understanding
why her brother acted as he did: "I know he can't help it, but doesn't
he see what this is doing to our parents?" Sensitive almost to a fault,
she admitted to being acutely aware of her parent's pain: how her
mother wiped her eyes with a tissue after each of Harry's outbursts;
how her father lit cigarette after cigarette, although trying to quit.
Karen's perspective, of course, is shaped by her experiences—the
need to compensate for her brother's feelings of persecution inside

the family. Not surprisingly, when Harry started to get healthy, Karen began to get worse. Once Harry was no longer dominating the home and family, Karen's neglected feelings began to surface, taking the form of resentment toward those who had ignored her for so long.

There are certainly factors over which children and their parents have little control. Unexpected tragedy and challenging circumstances such as illness, death, and parental job loss touch all families from time to time. What is important is that you are aware of the stressors *and* strengths unique to your family. Figure out what your family does well and do more of that. If your family loves Saturday pizza night, keep up that tradition. If you love following sports teams, don't stop. Maintaining your habits and traditions is important in the face of crisis. It helps your family preserve a sense of continuity, while the world you have known appears tenuous and unstable.

You won't be able to change everything, of course, but the story of Harry and his family illustrates how small environmental changes— asking Harry to take his own laundry to the basement, for example— can make a huge difference in how well your family relates to one another. If you cannot eradicate a particular source of tension, then do your best to work on your attitudes and ways of coping with that stress. Always remember, you are not helpless.

3. *Developmental Stage*

The developmental stage of a child or young adult will directly affect the way she views and interprets events. Mom "tagging along" on an outing may be fine if her daughter is ten, an embarrassment to the same child at fourteen, and a joy when the child is twenty-two. Nothing is different about what the mother is doing. It is the daughter's developmental stage that is changing.

Adolescence and young adulthood are known as periods of internal upheaval and shifting, as young people are in the process of "becoming." From about age twelve to the mid-twenties, a young woman will try on new behaviors and identities, sometimes as frequently as she tries on new clothes. If she finds a good "fit"—with certain behaviors, activities and friends well suited to her personality and temperament— then it is around these activities and people she may build a life. Although watching adult children distance themselves from us may go against our instincts, there is often little we can do other than to let them know we love and care for them. We do this by maintaining a level of contact that feels appropriate. Some parents will be tempted to intervene if they feel that their young person is too far off-track. There may be some wisdom to this strategy, but more often than not it is counterproductive. Children need time and space to acquire their independence.

There are at least two significant dangers in interrupting the natural processes of development: one, the young person may take longer to achieve her own sense of identity; and two, she may miss the opportunity to experience the consequences of her choices. More than once, I've been told by a young woman that her boyfriend was bad news and that she wanted to break up with him. In fact, she *would* break up with him, if only her parents would "lay off." This attitude is more than mere stubbornness. During adolescence the need for a young woman to differentiate herself from her parents is stronger than her need to exercise common sense and act in her own self-interest. As a result, when a young woman is challenged by her parents to end a destructive romantic relationship, she often stays in it months longer than she otherwise would.

The takeaway is that while a parent's influence is enormous, it is not complete. And that is as it should be. Despite the popular misconception, parents do not "mold" their children. In the best cases, a parent will help the child move a few steps forward in the direction of her gifts, and encourage her to overcome her unique set of challenges. The duty of the shy child's parents is to help her deal with her reticence. The aggressive child's parents must help her learn to manage emotional upheavals. The good parent does not "fix" a child who is broken or deficient, but serves as an essential resource to help the child develop as a person.

Happiness is indeed a conundrum. It is something we all want for our children, yet even the wealthiest among us cannot buy it. Attaining happiness is a constantly evolving process that involves a combination of one's temperament, environment, and responses to both. Our children may find it as a reward for the achievement of their goals or through self-acceptance, but it will not be found when a new Mini Cooper materializes, as if by magic, in the driveway.

CHAPTER THREE

The Paths to Anxiety

Many baby boomer women rightfully claim that compared to their own mothers they have "arrived." Their opportunities for education, professional achievement, and personal freedom far exceed anything their mothers might have dreamed possible. But while all of that is true, so is the unfortunate reality that when we get what we want, a whole new set of problems presents itself.

One of those difficulties—and one that is essential to understanding the parenting dilemmas faced by baby boomer mothers—is the anxiety that comes with increased choices. Having more choices means spending more time trying to make the right decisions and, as any woman who has tried to choose a birth control method or deliver a child can attest, that can feel overwhelming. The options baby boomer women have had at their disposal bear some review, as they are crucial to understanding their behavior as parents. Figure 3.1 is just a small sampling of the choices available to typical baby boomer mothers, as compared to their Depression-era counterparts.

Arguably one of the biggest differences between the generations lies in the availability of birth control. While Depression-era mothers were limited in their ability to control their reproduction, their daughters had the option of the birth control pill, intrauterine devices, and abortion, in addition to the traditional "rhythm" and "calendar" methods. Besides limited options for birth control, expectant mothers in the fifties and sixties had fewer choices in the

FIGURE 3.1 Mothers' Choices Across Child's Life Cycle

	Pre-boomer Moms	*Boomer and Post-boomer Moms*
Birth Control Options	· condoms · diaphragm · "rhythm method"	· birth control pills · abortion · intrauterine devices · condoms · diaphragm · "rhythm method" · birth control patches · injections
Prenatal and Birth Options	· hospital delivery · home delivery	· midwife, doula, surrogate mother, physician delivery · childbirth classes · birthing rooms · ultrasound · choice of gestational procedures · surgical options · music, books for the baby in utero · postponement of pregnancy
Infancy and Preschool	· stay at home, working only when needed	· stay at home, working part time or full time daycare and preschool choices · enrichment classes for babies, toddlers
Feed and Formulas	· cloth diapers · bottle feeding · breast feeding	· cloth diapers · disposable diapers · breast feeding · bottle feeding · formulas
School-age Children	· public school · private school	· public school · private school · home school · extracurricular activities · before- and after- school care

delivery room. By the time I gave birth to my first child in the late seventies, I was asked what kind of music I wanted during delivery, a question sure to have attracted looks of utter bewilderment just two decades earlier. From birthing centers and home births, to doulas, midwives, birthing coaches, and ultrasound, baby boomer mothers have had a host of options their mothers never had the opportunity to utilize.

As a baby grows and develops, decisions must be made as to the nature of his activities, the surroundings in which he will grow up, and the caregivers who will influence his intellectual and social development. Each of these is an important consideration that frequently falls on the mother. When one considers the enormous pressure baby boomer mothers faced to pursue a career, often while maintaining their role as the household's primary caregiver, it is no wonder so many of us became fraught with anxiety.

In the 1960s, while making important choices regarding their children's development, baby boomer mothers also had to decide whether to enter the workforce and, if so, to what extent. The human potential movement of this era, a social philosophy grounded in the belief that individuals had stores of unharnessed potential, saw record numbers of women attending college, many of them the first women in their families to earn a degree. Emboldened by the desire for a more fulfilling life and the rising tide of women's rights movement, young women, for the first time, had the encouragement and freedom to become whatever they pleased. The popularity of *Ms. Magazine* and its founder Gloria Steinem, the advent of "the pill," and the growing international recognition of women's reproductive rights were signs, however cautionary, that many of the former constraints on women's choices and behavior were eroding. Of course, this newfound freedom brought with it new obstacles. To some in the early feminist movement, working women who tried to do and be it all were revered, while stay-at-home moms were derided as hopelessly shackled. It was not until midway through the seventies that groups devoted to raising feminine consciousness appeared to help women recognize and cope with the realities of their greater options, and the real or anticipated opposition to these choices—guilt.

Educational Liberalism

More education usually leads to more liberal thinking, which in the sixties led to increased protests against whatever boomers disliked—war, materialism, racial injustice, and the list goes on. Baby boomers felt that they could make a difference. They felt in control. Generally, if a person feels in control of her capabilities and fate, her expectations follow suit. She will believe she can do anything. However, high expectations come with high anxiety, and while baby boomers got what they wanted in terms of greater education and opportunities, they also developed their share of neuroses. Time and again I see this in private practice; it is the achievers, those who feel they *should* be able to effect change, who land in therapy. Their perception of themselves as miracle workers able to correct any and all problems—including their children's—is unrealistic and bound to crumble.

In the realm of parenting, this tendency toward overconfidence on the part of boomers translates to exaggerated involvement in their children's lives. Parents who believe they should be involved in every aspect of their children's lives, from enrolling their children in Princeton Review SAT preparation courses to deciding on the color of their bed sheets, give fitting description to the word "micromanagement." Recently, there have been a number of news stories about hyper-involved parents who oversee their child's SAT preparation—and worse, parents who regularly intervene with college professors on their child's behalf. Such scrutiny and oversight was rarely the case during the Depression era. And it's not just test preparation and college admissions that have parents hovering over their children; it's every facet of their lives, to the point that parental involvement borders on obsession.

Of course every generation wants its children to fare well. The point is not that we should leave our children for the wolves, but that we need to be careful of responding slavishly to their every need. Learning is about making mistakes, and if we don't let our children make them we may be setting them on a dangerous course. Sometimes becoming overly involved in our children's educational lives is debilitating because it prompts our children to rely on us whenever they need a boost. And if that boost is an artificial one, it may set the child up for failure and disappointment later on.

Changing Family Structures and the Rise of Self-Help

Many of us would probably agree that significant social strides were made during the seventies and eighties. However, at the same time boomers began making meaningful social progress, the prospect of ever-increasing gratification brought difficult choices in the context of marriage. "Should I stay married?" "Am I being fulfilled in this relationship?" "I love him; I'm just not *in* love with him anymore." The growing belief that one's potential for happiness was boundless led to a significant increase in the rate of divorce and an increasing number of couples who no longer believed in staying together for the sake of their children. Suddenly new definitions of family—which included single parents, separated parents, blended families—became part of the national vocabulary. The media picked up on this shift and recast its portrayal of family life from homespun morality tales such as *Father Knows Best* and *Leave it to Beaver* to programs featuring dysfunctional families with silly, ineffectual fathers. At the same time, the nuclear family and extended family became increasingly distant, living in separate homes, often hundreds of miles apart. As they grew older, boomers came to rely less on their parents and in-laws for advice and the extended family lost relevance. Many families disintegrated and regrouped into new constellations. The architects of the family—the parents—were left without a clear blueprint to follow.

Who would step in to make sense of this and give the boomer generation guidance? Why, the professionals, of course! I like to refer to this trend as "Goodbye Intuition, Hello Experts." In the last thirty years, people have turned in ever-increasing numbers to spiritual gurus and self-help experts for advice on just about everything. The explosion of books on family life and personal improvement has been overwhelming—and not just for clients, but professionals as well. (Even therapists have a hard time keeping up with the seasonal influx of new titles). The more information that becomes available, much of it without empirical grounding, the greater the tendency for people to question their longstanding values and intuitive judgments. As parents, we must be wary of embracing every groundbreaking new theory that comes along, particularly those that don't feel right and lead us away from our instincts.

We have been witness to a radically changing world in the last fifty years. Multiple factors have converged on the baby boomer population as we have grown into adulthood—more education, a greater sense of autonomy and control, higher expectations of self, and above all, an erosion of traditional values. This combination has contributed to an anxiety unique to any American generation up till this point, and this anxiety, for worse not better, has dramatically influenced how we view ourselves as individuals and as parents.

- - - - - - - - - - - - - - - -

CHAPTER FOUR

Words of a Generation

The explosion of information and advice in the 1960s and 1970s brought with it dramatic changes in our language—not so much new words, as new significance to particular words and their frequency of use. In a culture increasingly preoccupied with fame and public perception, words such as humility, sacrifice, and modesty sharply declined in appearance, while words having to do with the self—*feelings* and *self-esteem*—steadily increased. (The Google Ngram Viewer tool allows the reader to trace the usage of any given word over time.)

With more leisure time, more money to spend, and more experts to consult about living, people were better equipped to focus on themselves. They were also more cognizant of the quality of their relationships with others. In this chapter, we'll explore three culturally esteemed words—*feelings*, *self-esteem*, and *relationships*—and the crucial role they play in how baby boomers see themselves and approach the world.

Relationships

We are a nation of relationship-obsessed people. We think about our relationships with our husbands and partners, our parents and in-laws, our significant others and friends. We think about relationships with people with whom we work and people in our neighborhood, and we worry about our children's relationships—with their friends, their boyfriends, their girlfriends and spouses, and above all, with us, their parents.

Recent research at the University of California, Los Angeles,[1] lends credence to the theory that parents are becoming increasingly connected to their older children, and that children do not mind the extra care and attention. In an evaluation of students' attitudes, the researchers found that most freshmen appreciated their parents' involvement in the college search. In fact, some students, especially those of Hispanic descent, reported they would have liked more involvement from their parents, in both applying to college and choosing classes.

Another significant trend is the increase in single-parent homes, from 10% of all U.S. homes in 1965, to 27% in 2001.[2] Adolescents in these homes are more likely to act as confidantes of their parents than those living in a dual-parent household, and at times the roles of the parents and their children can become blurred.

In preparation for writing this book, I interviewed dozens of middle to upper middle class women ages forty through sixty-five. The majority reported feeling closer to their adult children than to their own parents. They cited more and deeper conversations and more involvement in their children's lives. However, the results of my research have been mixed. While many of the women reported being satisfied with their relationships, a large minority cited room for improvement:

I want my son to be able to talk to me; I think we should "bond" more, share in activities together, have fun together. But he is quiet; he feels I am interrogating him when I ask questions. He wants me to leave him alone, but still give him one hundred percent support. I'm not supposed to be critical of him, but it's okay for him to take pot shots at me.

I want [my children] to have a relationship with me because they want to, not out of guilt. I want them to treat me like I treated my mother. But they talk to me like I would *never* have spoken to my mom.

My son wasn't answering my emails. I got tired of trying, so I got smart and wrote one with the following subject: "Re: Your inheritance." That got a response. It was my humorous attempt to keep the communication open.

My kids seem content in their relationship with me, but they don't like to see me get anxious. Then they talk less.

In some ways, the relationships we have with our children are intuitive. We feel as though we are good parents when the relationship feels right, and think we've done something wrong when the relationship is a struggle. When there is a rough patch in the relationship—and undoubtedly there will be—we blame ourselves first. Often we have done nothing wrong. In fact, friction may be a sign of something else entirely—an indication that the young adult is going through the age-appropriate business of emancipation.

Too often baby boomer parents sacrifice good judgment in favor of keeping the relationship on an even keel. When parents are put to the test by conflict the threat of separation may become too much to bear, and some adult children, knowing their parents' vulnerability when it comes to maintaining consistency in the relationship, take advantage. One mother, Amelia, a retired occupational therapist, explained it like this: "She [my daughter] was so good at sucking me in . . . because [she knows] I love my kids." Amelia was willing to put up with her daughter's rudeness rather than risk her daughter's disapproval. Another mother, Marilyn, told me she tolerates verbal abuse from her daughter in order to maintain contact with her grandsons. Unfortunately, this is a common characteristic of the parent–child relationship in the later years: grandchildren become a bartering tool the disgruntled adult child uses to claim power in the relationship. "You don't like what I'm saying? Well, you don't have to see *my* kids!"

In my research, parents and grandparents of baby boomers cared about how they got along with their children, but improving the quality of the relationship was less of a focus. Back in those days, relationship therapy, support groups, and relationship classes and coaches didn't exist. Surely parents had struggles with their children and suffered when the relationships did, but this suffering was often done quietly. As one of seven children in a Russian Orthodox family, my mother assumed hers had a "normal" amount of conflict for one that size. To my knowledge, she spent little, if any, time hashing and rehashing the intricacies of her family dynamics.

By contrast, there is a marked self-consciousness to the way in which baby boomers approach these relationships. It is as if every thought and nuance of feeling is subject to scrupulous evaluation. We know people whose relationships "just aren't working;" people who are "in an open relationship;" people who have "toxic relationships" with their in-laws, coworkers, neighbors, or families. There are relationship therapists and coaches; classes and workshops on how to enhance our relationships; books and websites devoted to mending, healing, improving, re-energizing, and beginning and ending them. Pick up nearly any women's magazine, and you'll be sure to encounter advice on how to improve at least one type of relationship in your life.

But what is wrong with wanting to improve our relationships? My point is not to be critical of our generation, but rather to point to the tremendous desire and self-imposed pressures baby boomers feel to connect with their children. The simple word "relationship" carries with it much more weight and expectation than it did for prior generations. Too often parents feel an exaggerated responsibility to nurture the relational bond, sometimes to the point of becoming the desperate "pursuer" whose affection goes unreturned. Remember, wanting a quality relationship and actually having one are not the same. Your child must also play an active role in strengthening the connection.

Feelings

We baby boomers, as a rule, believe in the supremacy of our feelings. We want to understand how we feel; what we feel; how we can feel better, and the list goes on. As children, many of us repeated the saying, "Sticks and stones may break my bones, but names can never hurt me": our parents' version of a relationship course. Simplistic? Yes, but the message was clear. Don't become a victim of the names you may be called. Names are just words. The survivors of the Great Depression, having suffered in their own right, wanted to equip their children with the necessary toughness to survive the inevitable travails of growing up. At times our parents may have seemed short on empathy, but their intent was honorable.

However, at some point between then and now, an offense to our feelings came to be seen as extremely damaging. Rather than simply sloughing off the names, we are encouraged to recognize, identify, and express the embarrassment and pain resulting from another's behavior towards us. Generally, this is a good thing. It helps us make sense of our life experiences. If we can know and understand ourselves, then we are in a better position to respond to others. But lately I worry that feelings have assumed too much importance. During therapy sessions, I often hear people say, in reference to a family member: "He hurt my feelings," or, "What about my feelings?" It is as if a person's feelings are unimpeachable, a special domain not to be questioned in any way.

This uncritical view of feelings has gained traction in American courtrooms, where people routinely sue one another for damages resulting from emotional injuries. At times, this is appropriate, but what about in our personal relationships and interactions with family and friends? We need a better recourse than seeking litigation whenever our feelings are hurt. To live is to hurt. It is essential that this be understood. Without this recognition, honest communication will cease to occur.

Acknowledging there may be discomfort when we discuss our feelings with loved ones helps reframe the discussion. When the hurt person can see that her pain is momentary, a small part of a larger and more holistic process, it becomes easier to endure. To use an analogy from the field of women's medicine: knowing we will experience discomfort during a mammogram is tolerable, if we can see beyond the pain to the eventual benefits.

Fortunately, in many loving relationships, the conversation doesn't automatically stop whenever one's feelings are hurt. In healthy families, once parents and their children are able to move past the difficulty inherent in painful conversations, the caring each has for the other, as well as the desire to minimize harm, creates an environment conducive for recovery. According to the author Janis Abrahms Spring, a person usually needs a witness, someone to "hold" his hurt feelings, in order to let them go. In *After the Affair*,[3] she discusses this idea in the context of adultery, encouraging the hurt partner to let the unfaithful partner hold her feelings, as a step toward releasing them. Her notion of "holding," however, applies to many situations. We see "holding" at work in counseling. Therapists help clients release hurt feelings by allowing for their expression and acknowledging the validity of the feelings. Family members and friends can do the same for one another.

Sometimes, however, the feelings people carry with them are the result of interactions from earlier in their lives, disturbing events that have never been adequately resolved. Since it is not always possible for people to take care of unfinished business with past acquaintances and estranged relatives, therapists work with their clients in a variety of ways to assist them. In addition to recognizing, identifying, and expressing their feelings, clients need a way to let negative feelings go. Sometimes the very act of expressing feelings is sufficient to release them, but often our emotions are more complex than that. Changing the tenor of an individual's feelings is a daunting task for a therapist, especially when these feelings are interwoven within the fabric of the person's belief system. One treatment model known as cognitive behavioral therapy suggests that a person's thoughts or beliefs will determine how she feels. If thoughts or beliefs become distorted ("I must be perfect in order to be loved"; "If I feel foolish in a situation, I must be a fool"; "Good mothers *always* put themselves last"), they can become reflexive and result in depression and anxiety. Fortunately, learning to modify and correct those thoughts often results in a lessening of symptoms—which, for the client, is both empowering and freeing.

When we love someone, we are typically more sensitive to their opinions and more vulnerable to being hurt. In some situations, adult children take advantage of the parent's desire for a good relationship and may use words or actions as weapons to purposely injure. This is not healthy on the adult child's part, and it certainly is not healthy for the parent. I have known parents, for instance, whose adult children behave in extremely hateful ways, to the point of attacking them with accusations that are exaggerated, distorted, or blatantly false. I call this "rewriting the family history." The danger is that if such wild accusations are heard often enough, parents come to view them as true. The adult child then repeats their revisionist version of events in an effort to inflict emotional abuse. No parent should have to experience that, but many do, because they feel responsible at some level for their child's actions. They desperately want to maintain goodwill in the relationship, so they sacrifice their sanity and health.

One could make the argument, convincingly in my view, that parents in the United States have reached a level of unprecedented tolerance for backtalk from their children. Assuming for a moment that that is true, some of this laxity is no doubt due to the parental belief that children should be free to express themselves without the threat of criticism or punishment, both of which may damage their children's self-esteem. It is true that many preadolescents and adolescents purposely make irritating and inflammatory remarks to their parents as a part of the separation and individuation process. However, when children are expressing their views with the sole intent of insulting or abusing their parents, parents need to take notice.

We all have the challenge of helping our children learn how to manage their emotional lives. That includes helping them understand not just how someone may have "made" them feel, but how others—including their mother or father—feel as a result of their language and actions.

Self-Esteem

One of the most heavily laden words of our time is "self-esteem." We want it, and we want our kids to have it. And although we can't observe it in the same way we observe someone's eye color, we can guess who has it by subtler clues: one's posture, speech patterns, and choice of clothing. Parents have always wanted their children to have confidence, but prior to the baby boomer generation, self-esteem books, therapy groups, and feeling-based workshops were virtually unheard of. How then did self-esteem become a national preoccupation?

Although there is no single answer, part of the reason lies in several major cultural shifts that occurred during baby boomers' lifetimes, including a higher rate of divorce, more blended families, a greater percentage of single parents, and more mothers working outside the home. Taken together, these trends have led to an environment in which more children are being left in the care of others or unsupervised.

The shifting pedagogical expectations of public education also play a vital role. Once focused primarily on the three Rs—reading, writing and arithmetic—schools in the United States, beginning in the early 1970s, have gradually broadened their focus so that the "whole child" is considered when designing curricula. As increasing numbers of children were deemed in need of emotional and social support, public schools began taking on more responsibility for children's development, including the development of their self-esteem. The prevailing wisdom was that praise, reinforcement, and encouragement were among the major factors leading to a positive self-image. Educators who were a part of the whole language movement believed that good self-esteem would result in improved school performance and lowered rates of pregnancy, delinquency, and drug use. Programs and entire curriculums were developed to enhance how a child felt about himself.

At the same time, boomer parents became increasingly concerned with their children's self-image. For the most part, this concern has been beneficial. Parents have become more careful about the ways in which they speak to their children. We have learned to express our disappointment about a *behavior*, not about the *child himself*. But, as with all progress, there is a downside to all of this. With the heightened focus on self-esteem, many parents now worry they will do permanent damage to their children by setting limits and holding their children accountable to even modest standards of behavior and speech. Some are reluctant to discipline their children for fear of bruising their children's egos. Unfortunately, this has led to the raising of tyrants—not always, but enough to alter the generational dynamics of the parent-child relationship.

Roy Baumeister, a social psychologist at Florida State University, has extensively reviewed self-esteem studies, focusing his attention on the connection between achievement and self-esteem. As he reported in May 2003, in the journal *Psychological Science in the Public Interest*,[4] programs encouraging a student to feel good about himself, regardless of his grades, sometimes take away that student's motivation to do his best. In fact, one study suggested that boosting a student's self-esteem without delivering a message of personal responsibility weakened scholastic performance. While improved performance in school will likely increase self-esteem, the converse is not necessarily true: enhanced self-esteem is no guarantee a student will perform any better.

A good case can be made that U.S. students attending college in the twenty-first century have received more praise and encouragement than any generation before them. The result is not what one might expect. Professor Jean Twenge of San Diego State University was one of five psychologists authoring a study about college students and self-esteem. In the study, the researchers examined the responses of more than 16,000 students nationwide on the Narcissistic Personality Inventory. What they discovered was that, although students appear to be more assertive and confident than ever, their scores also suggest they are more self-centered and "entitled" than their predecessors. Twenge and her colleagues express concern that these young people may be at greater risk of difficulties with empathy in their relationships with others. In her 2009 book, *The Narcissism Epidemic: Living in the Age of Entitlement*,[5] she contends that the spread of narcissism is a destructive cultural force, that raising children to feel exceptional and entitled is not only bad for the children but for the culture at large. With convincing evidence to support her position, Twenge offers a "treatment" plan for curbing the epidemic: namely, reducing the "amount of attention paid to self-admiration and self-expression" and increasing "the attention paid to our common American cultural ideals, such as freedom, self-reliance, and equality."[6]

Beyond the obvious—that raising a generation of narcissists is not in parents' best interest—what does all this mean? One of the biggest worries of parents of young adults with entitlement issues is that their children will not look after them in their later years. The jury is still out, but it is quite possible these parents' fears are well-grounded.

Despite the efforts of parents and schools, self-esteem does not necessarily come easily. Some people are hard on themselves from a young age, and even with success and a supportive family, they do not have a great deal of confidence. Therapists frequently see people who, on the surface, appear quite successful and "together." Yet, these same individuals think if others *truly* knew them, they would discover inadequacies. These people often are described as having the "imposter syndrome."[7] They feel like phonies, no matter their accomplishments.

The good news is that it is never too late to improve one's self-image. We are always in the process of becoming. Countless people with low self-esteem have learned to challenge their beliefs about themselves and replace those insecurities with more accurate, self-affirming depictions. They have done so by moving out of their comfort zones, trying out new and healthier behaviors, and redefining what success means to them. With effort there is always the possibility of changing ourselves.

CHAPTER FIVE

Handling Guilt

How Perfect Do We Have to Be?

Guilt is a time-honored tradition shared by many mothers. No matter how slight or severe the circumstance, mothers never fail to find themselves worthy of blame. There is guilt for doing too much and guilt for doing too little, guilt for leaving the home to work and guilt for staying home to manage domestic duties, guilt for getting a divorce and guilt for staying married. Some mothers feel guilty whenever their adult children are upset with them. Regardless of the circumstance, there seems to be plenty of guilt to go around, and plenty of mothers willing to accept it.

In the Judeo-Christian heritage, the notion of a gender-specific guilt burden begins with Eve's temptation of Adam in the Old Testament. Her proffering of the apple resulted in banishment from the Garden of Eden and, according to some, the fall of mankind. Throughout history women have been alternately praised for their purity and virtue and decried as villains, witches, and whores. Since the vast majority of early writings were authored by men in seats of power and influence, their views tended to dominate the discussion.

Professionals in the twentieth century only added fuel to the fire, roundly criticizing mothers for the difficulties endured by their children and even holding mothers responsible for conditions such as childhood autism. Child psychologist Bruno Bettelheim, in the 1960s, picked up on what psychiatrist Leo Kanner earlier had described as the "cold perfection[ism]" of parents of children with autism.[1] Usually a defender of parents, Kanner said autistic children were "kept neatly in a refrigerator which didn't defrost," his remarks ushering in the "Refrigerator Mother" theory of autism—that a mother's coldness was responsible for the condition. Bettelheim went on to write *The Empty Fortress: Infantile Autism and the Birth of the Self*,[2] a popular 1967 book which at one point compares autistic children to concentration camp prisoners held captive by unfeeling SS guards. Bettelheim claimed that infants of cold mothers were left with no choice but extreme withdrawal. Advances in research have long since debunked his theory, but its legacy is apparent in the exaggerated sense of responsibility many mothers feel for their children's well-being.

More recently, we've seen a generational influence on the prevalence and severity of maternal guilt. Baby boomer mothers tend to exercise a more hands-on approach to parenting than their Depression-era predecessors. They meet the challenge of parenting just like other projects they take on—with an armful of self-help books, guidance from professionals in the field, and the belief that with the right resources they can solve any problem. Compared to their parents, they have more knowledge and skills, but they also have more anxiety.

American author and physician Andrew Weil documents a generational difference, for instance, in how women account for the development of breast cancer. In prior generations, women were more likely to blame breast cancer on external factors, not always based in sound medical evidence (one supposed culprit was collision with a steering wheel). Today women are more likely to heap blame on themselves, citing stress and emotional repression as two of the main causes of the disease.[3]

Healthy Versus Unhealthy Guilt

June Tangney and Ronda Dearing describe guilt as one of the "self-conscious emotions."[4] In their enlightening 2002 release *Shame and Guilt*, the authors distinguish "self-conscious" emotions, such as guilt and shame, from "basic" feelings, such as joy, anger, and fear. People of any age can experience the basic emotions, Tangney and Dearing claim, but the self-conscious emotions require a person to have a sense of self as separate from others. Children as young as two can be embarrassed, and toddlers can have a very rudimentary sense of right and wrong. But it is not until later that children understand the severity of their behavior and their personal responsibility for it.

Young children will feel guilt with regard to concrete actions, such as breaking a mother's vase, but only in adolescence and adulthood will they experience guilt in a relational context—feeling acute remorse for cheating on a spouse, for example.

It is important to keep in mind that guilt has a purpose, and healthy levels of guilt support behaviors needed to maintain civilized societies. People feel a pang of anticipatory guilt at the idea of stealing from a neighbor, and this uneasiness prevents them from acting on the urge. From a parenting standpoint, allowing your child to experience a modest level of guilt can help him distinguish right from wrong.

Here it is worth pausing to distinguish between guilt and shame. The latter, common in traditional Japan and well explained by Tangney and Dearing, is more global than guilt and involves a negative assessment of the self. While guilt is usually specific to a behavior or thought, shame can consume one's entire identity and lead to social ostracism. Someone may experience tension, remorse, and regret as part of feeling guilty, but the experience of shame is further reaching. Feeling small, worthless, and powerless are all components of shame.

The practice of shaming dates back to the days of the Japanese samurai, from the eleventh to fourteenth century. Back then, if the samurai lost his honor, his only way to eradicate his shame was seppuku, the act of ritual suicide by disembowelment. As Ruth Benedict, author of the World War II-era study of Western and Japanese cultures, *The Chrysanthemum and the Sword*,[5] remarks, "shame cultures rely on external sanctions for good behavior, not, as true guilt cultures do, on an internalized conviction of sin." In other words, shame is a response to other people's criticism, and, accordingly, honoring the larger group becomes more important than protecting one's individual feelings.

The main lesson is that, while some guilt may be healthy, too much can be debilitating, particularly when it lingers and leads one to doubt his self-worth. If you forget about a lunch date with a friend and feel bad about it, you'll likely experience some low-level guilt. The healthy response is to call your friend, apologize, and make plans to reconnect. The unhealthy response—shame—is to lose sleep over the error and conclude you are a horrible friend. Shame takes many forms. Perceived mistakes that leave you feeling worthless as a parent, undeserving of love, are indicators of shame. Any time your self-conception is injured and you want to shrink or hide, you are experiencing shame. These feelings deserve further investigation and, in some cases, professional help.

Three Types of Guilt

Generally, guilt falls into one of three categories: (1) the discomfort a person feels about his feelings toward others, (2) the negative perception a person has about his own behavior, or (3) the responsibility a person feels for the behavior of someone else. Let's explore these now.

Guilt for Negative Feelings toward Others

Whenever you have a thought you don't like, you may be tempted to criticize yourself as uncaring, selfish, or mean. It is natural to feel guilty for having such thoughts, but be careful how you go about dealing with them. More often than not, trying to banish a negative thought backfires. Parents are especially vulnerable to this kind of guilt. We think that we *should* feel positive towards our children, regardless of their ages or conduct. To help moderate that feeling, here are a few ideas to keep in mind:

1. Normalize your negative thoughts and feelings.

Recognize that it is indeed normal to have negative thoughts at times. You might love your adult child's spouse, yet secretly yearn for that spouse to disappear for a week or two, so that you can have your child all to yourself. You might love your brother, but dread visiting him because his much larger house leaves you feeling envious. In small doses, these feelings are natural, but it is important not to let them seep into resentment.

2. Strive to understand your negative thoughts or feelings.

You can learn a great deal about yourself when you understand your feelings and their origins. Do you remember how you helped your children express and understand their feelings? Maybe you pride yourself on being positive and don't want others to know that you are capable of pessimism and depression. By tracking the development of your thinking, you can look more objectively at what cognitive behavioral therapists call "cognitive distortions" and learn to replace negative thoughts with more optimistic ones.

3. There is a huge difference between a "bad thought" and a bad action.

The guilt parents feel for having a "bad thought" is often as strong as if they'd acted on it. Remember, negative thoughts kept to yourself do not hurt anyone but you. You will feel much better, in fact, if you can train yourself to accept and acknowledge your unwanted thoughts. Left to accumulate, these ideas can quickly lead to depression and anger, which can hurt you and those you relate to.

One way to get rid of unwanted thoughts is to "resist resisting them." Instead of criticizing yourself for your thoughts, become an observer. Think of an island hut, shuttered on all sides. If a strong breeze comes along when the shutters are closed, the hut will be buffeted by the breeze. But when the shutters are open, air can flow through. The same is true when you are having a negative thought. When you stop criticizing yourself and become mindful of your inner dialogue ("I'm aware that I'm terribly jealous of my daughter's freedom and youthfulness"), you open the shutters and allow troubling thoughts to pass. Becoming comfortable with such a Zen-like approach is not easy. It requires time and practice to detach from one's thoughts and view them as ephemeral.

Keep in mind that too much isolation—especially for those who tend to engage in prolonged introspection—may be dangerous. Whenever we keep thoughts entirely to ourselves, we run the risk of their becoming distorted, losing perspective as our brain becomes an echo chamber. Cognitive therapists know this and help people identify thoughts or beliefs that are inaccurate. They use a variety of terms to describe such thoughts: "irrational beliefs," "dysfunctional thoughts," and "cognitive distortions"[6]: These impact how one feels and consequently how one meets the world. Physician and author Daniel Amen contends that our thoughts, which are often automatic, don't always tell the truth, yet we may behave as if they are accurate.[7] Such negative thoughts affect not only our emotional health but also our bodies, relationships, and sense of personal power. A person with such habits of the mind may look at the world in purely black and white terms, ignoring all positive aspects of a given situation and predicting the worst possible outcome.

People don't come by these irrational thoughts overnight. They build over time and take up increasing amounts of mental space. Being able to identify and recognize unhealthy thoughts is the first step. Then the individual must replace them with more balanced, realistic ones about himself in relation to others. New messages to the self can and do allow us to take charge of how we feel.

Guilt for Our Behavior and Actions

The second type of guilt comes largely as a result of our own actions, although, at times, we may have a distorted view of how harmful these actions really are. Here are a few things to consider:

1. Are your expectations of yourself realistic?

You may be more troubled by your behavior than are others in your life. Consult with your spouse or a close friend to see how they feel about what you have (or haven't) done. In talking to them, you may find that your guilt isn't warranted. Many adult children have unrealistically high expectations of their parents. It is amazing how a parent can come to believe unfounded criticism, if that criticism is repeated often enough.

2. Feelings hold elevated status in our culture.

One of the most common causes of guilt is the perception that a person's feelings have been slighted. Women seem especially prone to feeling guilty when they think their actions may have hurt another's feelings. Keep in mind that avoiding criticism or dissatisfaction may jeopardize the opportunity you have for real communication. In fact, pleasing others can be the antithesis of good mental health, if that "pleasing" is at odds with your true feelings.

3. Your child or friend may not forgive you, despite your best effort to make amends.

If you've offended your child, if you think what you've done warrants apology, do your best to make amends. But realize that is all you can do. Some people forgive easily. Others do not. Relationships sometimes *are* altered forever. With or without reconciliation, we must seek ways to move on.

Guilt for the Behaviors of Others

The third type of guilt, perhaps the most irrational, is the guilt we feel for the behavior of others. Short of brute force, we cannot *make* another person do something. Yet feeling guilty about our adult children's behavior is what many of us often do, identifying too closely with our children and not establishing clear boundaries. The next time you blame yourself for something your child said or did, consider that he may be subtly influencing how you perceive the situation. Here are some additional matters to consider:

1. *Feeling guilty is automatic for some parents.*

Because guilt is such a strong emotion, the delusions it produces *feel* real, and we tend to accept them on the basis of their strength alone. Individuals who experience intense guilt often use the word "should." "I should have done a better job teaching Emily to write thank-you notes," or "I should have done more to warn Chad about marijuana." Never mind that Emily's parents spoke with her at the kitchen table the day after Christmas, prompting her to begin work on her thank-you notes, or that Chad's parents had their son in counseling throughout his teenage years. The mistaken belief of these parents is that all the shortcomings of their children are a result of poor parenting.

2. *Manipulative adult children will make attempts to reinforce their parents' guilt.*

Adult children who are stuck in their own development may place undue blame on their parents in an attempt to induce guilt. Because boundaries with their parents have not been well established, they believe they may hold their parents responsible for their own mistakes. Young adults who yell the loudest about having controlling parents are frequently the least willing to assume control of their own emotions and actions. Confronted with insults and accusations, parents are immobilized, convinced of their own guilt for made-up offenses.

3. *Setting appropriate boundaries will influence your child's behavior.*

When your child shows a lack of respect, your best, and often only, option is to figure out how you may be unconsciously resisting appropriate boundaries. To set limits on your child's behavior, use assertive language that holds him accountable, and clarify your role in the situation. As a starting point, the mother of a son returning to drug treatment might say something like, "Chad, I'm sorry that your choices landed you back in rehab. I will be supportive of your sobriety in any way I can." However, if Chad then screams at her, claiming his drug use is her fault, she should remain firm: "I'd be glad to talk about how we can work together better now, but I'll need to hang up the phone if you continue to scream at me." If the screaming continues, Chad's mother should hang up.

4. *Your standards for yourself are likely higher than those you have for others.*

If your child is holding you to unrealistic expectations, talk to others to get a healthy perspective. Consider that your negative thoughts about yourself, while automatic, may not be accurate. The mother who personalizes everything needs to reevaluate her ability to influence others. The mind-reading father needs to accept that he does not automatically know what others are thinking and that communication may be more effective than intuition in arriving at the truth.

The wonderful thing about exploring our own thoughts and feelings is that doing so creates an opportunity for a kinder and more forgiving understanding of ourselves. Accurately assessing the limits of our responsibility allows us to be more assertive. And becoming more assertive in this context—with our adult children—communicates self-respect, enhances the establishment of boundaries, and puts responsibility for our children's behavior where it belongs: on them. When we feel grounded in who we are, we will be stronger in each of our relationships.

PART TWO

The Dance of Differentiation

CHAPTER SIX

Separation and Individuation
What's Good, Normal, and Healthy

The major developmental task of adolescence and early adulthood is called "separation and individuation." During this period, the young person finds ways to develop his own identity and distinguish himself from his parents. In some families, separation and individuation happens fairly smoothly. In others, it drags on into the child's twenties and thirties.

I like to call the separation and individuation process the dance of differentiation. It requires at least two partners, the parent and the child, who must take turns leading, alternating their movements to accord with the music. This dance can have a smooth, waltz-like pace or accelerate into frenzy; the dancers can hold one another close or remain at a distance. Whatever steps are taken, the hope is by the end of the dance the partners will have a mutual respect for one another.

While parents generally want their children to become independent, many do not welcome the dissension that may come as part of the process. The good news is this period is temporary and transitional and, generally, healthy. Even so, it can be difficult. Textbooks on adolescent and young adult development often compare the adolescent years to the "terrible twos" because the same developmental process is at hand. This comparison goes back to the work of the psychoanalyst Margaret Mahler,[1] who applied separation and individuation theory as a framework to explain normal child development. Over time, Mahler reasoned, very young children gradually differentiate from their parents. At about five months of age an infant is aware of his mother, for example, but lacks a sense of individuality. By the time he is a toddler, he begins to realize that he is a separate person from her, a recognition that is both exciting and frightening. Later, as the child acquires language—especially the word "no"—he begins to feel power. This stage can be especially frustrating for parents, as the child often will send mixed signals. One day he may relish being held and babied. The next he may scream "no" when his mother lends a hand to help him dress. Parents throw up their hands in frustration, for it seems however they respond, the child will continue to be grouchy and displeased. It is no wonder that books written about this developmental period include titles such as *Your Two-Year-Old: Terrible or Tender* and *Your Three-Year-Old: Friend or Enemy*.[2] And as many parents will attest, the teenage years are often just as volatile, as adolescents are primed to test their parents.

Of course it is a difficult time for children, as well. During adolescence the young person is preparing for the final separation from his parents, the one which marks his emotional entry into adulthood. Some teenagers may feel awkward about having their parents chaperone them to a dance. Others may go through a period of not even wanting to be seen with their parents—which, predictably perhaps, leads parents to try to get more involved. The result of this involvement in most cases is the teenager's attempt to retreat, to claim his or her territory as an individual.

Whether it's tattoos and piercings, questionable choices in friends, or other acts of rebellion, adolescents have plenty of methods at their disposal to demonstrate to us that they will not readily conform to our lifestyle and values. The clinical psychologist Anthony Wolf notes in his very funny book *Get Out of My Life, But First Can You Drive Me and Cheryl to the Mall?*[3] that many teens purposely push parents away, in an effort to convince themselves of their independence. Wolf is among those who claim, rightly, that the more dependent a young person feels, the greater the degree to which she will challenge her parents. At the beginning of adolescence, a young woman may interpret a parent's care and concern as an attempt to treat her like a child. Once she has completed the emancipation process, she will be much less likely to be embarrassed by innocent comments from her parents.

The gradual process of emancipation often starts around age eleven, when previously compliant children often become willful and insubordinate. A mother and father may panic when their son suddenly begins questioning their rules about his bedtime and his responsibility to feed the family dog. Fearful of ending up with a rebellious teenager, they clamp down on the child by grounding him and restricting his access to video games. It is quite a moment, however, when their son realizes his parents cannot make him do things. This is new territory for the boy, and for his parents who must realize they do not control their son. Yet while the parents may not have control, they do have leverage. Smart parents recognize this and know the value of negotiating differences, working toward compromise, and, most of all, listening. On the other hand, parents accustomed to using phrases such as "because I told you so" may need to rethink their script. Authoritarian rule must give way to a more open dialogue, if there is to be harmony in the household.

Of course not every area of disagreement with a teenager requires attention, resolution, or a specific consequence, and parents who feel they must win every battle will have great difficulty earning their children's trust and respect. Accepting the healthy premise of a child's need to differentiate means understanding there will be areas in which your views and opinions will not prevail. Admitting you are human, refraining from having the last word in every argument, goes a long way in communicating to a child that his separate views can be heard with respect. Even if he does not ultimately get his way on a particular matter, it is good, for all involved, that his opinion has been heard and validated.

The Function of Friction: Separation and Individuation into Adulthood

Most people have known a promising, intellectually capable adult who has never left his parents' home. It may be because there was little to no intergenerational friction. The emancipation process is a bumpy ride, and friction between the parent and child is often the impetus that results in the young person's decision to leave home. One family's final straw was the stepmother's refusal to allow her stepson to use an old saxophone she kept in the attic. The instrument had sentimental value to the stepmother, who, aware of the cavalier way in which her stepson treated items borrowed from others, simply refused his request. Her husband, the child's biological father, refused to take sides. He was shocked, however, when his twenty-year-old son announced that he had "had it" with them both and was moving in with his best friend. Initially, the father was upset with his wife, but soon after his son had left the home, he was pleasantly surprised to see how much better they all got along. Who would have guessed that a saxophone would be the catalyst for this young man's emancipation?

The time during which an adolescent is progressing through stages of separation and individuation can be one of the most unrewarding periods of parenting. On the one hand, parents are expected to relinquish control. At the same time, they are concerned the result may be disastrous—the values they have been promoting for years may be all for naught, once the child is set free. A teenager undoubtedly will make challenging statements as he tries out his emerging sense of self. This is part of the individuation process and should not be a cause for alarm. It is best to acknowledge the child's viewpoint, while feeling free to state yours.

When a sixteen-year-old daughter challenges her mother's rules by going to a forbidden party and drinking, her mother worries, fearing her daughter is rejecting years of moral teachings. Really, her daughter may be quite content with the values her parents have instilled. The decision is simply her way of pushing for more independence. The mother's job, in this case, is to understand the dynamics of the situation and react appropriately, providing proper guidance as to the risks of such behavior (e.g., underage drinking can lower inhibitions, lead to risky sexual behavior, or land you in jail) and determining appropriate consequences, without taking all this too personally. To a parent, an adolescent's disobedience may seem like a personal affront; however, there is a larger phenomenon at work here: the need for the child to claim ownership of her choices.

Now suppose that same daughter moves out of state to attend college or take a new job. Here again, she is engaging in the process of emancipation. While her parents may expect daily phone contact, she may have other ideas: her life as a young woman may include the desire for privacy and more distance from her parents. Returning home between semesters, she may have a new view on politics, or a new preference for the type of young man she likes to date. A good parent will do more listening and less intervening, recognizing the changes in her daughter as a natural part of growth and emancipation.

In any household, there are times when tensions run high. Parents often assume such conflict foreshadows things to come. Mothers, especially, fear not having an idealized relationship with their daughters, one in which they can go out together for lunches and shopping excursions and, later, develop close bonds through their grandchildren. However, the fear that animosity and rebellion in the teenage years will continue into adulthood is usually unjustified. The circumstances may never be perfect, but it is only by tolerating separation that a parent and her child may later develop a meaningful adult relationship.

Still, parents of the baby boomer generation are right in their acknowledgment of the unique difficulties members of their generation confront in guiding their children through the separation and individuation process. In the twenty-first century, adolescence, as a developmental stage, seems to be taking longer than ever before. Many universities recognize this trend and at least one has incorporated an explanation of the individuation process into its departmental mission statement. The Psychological and Counseling Center at Vanderbilt University reports that many students experience difficulty "establishing their autonomy and developing confidence in their ability to handle change."[4] They list fifteen true or false statements reflecting some of the most common issues students deal with in their path toward emancipation (e.g., "My family is more involved in my life than I prefer"; "I fear distance from those I care about"). Interestingly, the Center's website notes that some of those with difficulty separating from their parents are coming from homes where things are not "okay." Students who fit this category show responses such as, "I feel I should be at home to take care of things there"; "It is hard not to worry about things at home that I cannot change."

No parent can guarantee an untroubled life for her emerging young adult, and it is not unusual for stresses at home to impact the separation and individuation process. Below are some common indicators of an ongoing emancipation process. Consider these factors when thinking about the behavior of your own child:

1. Increased friction in conversation
2. Change in the pattern of contact
3. Need for greater privacy in his or her life
4. Less disclosure to parents
5. Hypercriticism toward parents
6. Hypersensitivity to parental feedback

The important thing to remember is that these behaviors tell us there may be something healthy going on in our children, rather than something problematic. How you know for certain is a matter for your own reflection and consideration. A young woman in college may stop the daily calls to her mother and reduce the frequency of e-mails as part of turning to her peers for more support. That likely isn't cause for alarm. But if she blocks e-mails and Facebook from her parents and refuses to return calls in what appears to be a severing of ties, parents are right to be concerned. Similarly, wanting more privacy in her life is normal; she may not share the details of her romantic relationships as she had in high school. But if she refuses to tell her parents anything about the guy she is seeing and never introduces him although he lives in the same city, that may be a red flag. As parents, it is your job to interpret the signals you are receiving, on the basis of the *extent and degree* of the behaviors. Before jumping to any conclusion, consider the normal developmental dynamics that are in play.

Parallels in Parent Development

Just as teens or young adults may give mixed signals to their parents, so too may parents give such signals to their children. Young adults bristle when their parents treat them as mature, responsible individuals one day and then hover over them the next, scrutinizing the way they do their laundry or comb their hair. The conflicted message parents are sending to their adult children in such instances is, "Be independent, but you're still my baby."

And letting go of our children produces both excitement and trepidation. We are delighted to see a son or daughter get "launched" in life, but fearful of the challenges we know that life will bring. The knowledge that the relationship we have with our children is changing can be—and often is—a source of tremendous anxiety, as we must find new ways of interacting with our children and often with each other as parents. Here are some suggestions for easing the frustration that frequently accompanies this difficult period of our children's development.

1. Accept separation and individuation as normal and healthy.

2. Do not "guilt" your adult children into being with you.

3. Show that you respect your children's "right" to their own views by listening and acknowledging them.

4. Do more listening than questioning.

5. Recognize that your children's criticism of you frequently serves a larger purpose; try not to take it personally.

6. Recognize that hypersensitivity can be an indicator that your son or daughter still needs your approval and is uneasy about not getting it.

There is no one best way for a young person to emancipate, nor a single timeline in which the process of differentiation will occur. Individual, family, and cultural differences all play a part in one's transition into adulthood, and the process will vary greatly in the level of stress it provokes in the family. While some families appear to glide through these transitions, others are challenged to their very core. Your family will have its own unique way of navigating through this stage of family life. In the next chapter, we will continue to explore differentiation, taking at a closer look at what shapes this delicate, wonderfully improvised dance.

CHAPTER SEVEN

The Adult Child's Temperament and Environment

We've all heard the adage "no person develops in a vacuum," and it has stuck around for a reason. Temperament, one's physical and emotional wiring, has a powerful influence on a young person's ability and willingness to separate and individuate. But environmental influences such as a child's chronic illness or a parent's death or divorce also play a vital role, as do our decisions as parents. To understand what techniques will be most useful in motivating our children to become self-sufficient, we must look at how all of these factors intersect to shape a child's development.

Understanding Your Child

Temperament has a profound effect on how we meet life. From the extreme introvert to the socially graceful extrovert, young adults vary remarkably in their inclinations toward human interaction. But knowing where a child falls on the spectrum does not make it easier to predict how well he will progress through the process of separation and individuation: a gregarious extrovert may have just as much difficulty emancipating from his parents as his introverted cousin.

Take Phil, the youngest of five children in a Phoenix suburb. The young man had the near-constant look of someone who had just gotten out of bed. His father Gerald left home at seventeen, married at eighteen, and proceeded directly into the world of work and parenting. When Phil turned seventeen, his father knew it was time to have a talk with his son about the young man's plans for the future. Gerald's expectation was that, at eighteen, the summer after high school graduation, Phil would move into his own apartment. That is what he had done, after all, and it was also the path followed by his other children. More to the point, Gerald was looking forward, at least privately, to a shrinking household and the day he would be alone with his wife. The problem was that he ignored the clues Phil had been leaving for years. Phil had never attended a single school-sponsored social event in his four years of high school. He had one close friend from church, and only reluctantly participated in the community service and charity events the church hosted. Perhaps most telling, however, was Phil's complete lack of interest in learning to drive. He was content to have his friend pick him up and take him wherever the two would go, often a nearby video game store, which carried the latest games.

About four weeks shy of graduation, Phil's father asked him about his plans to move out. Phil had none. This, of course, was unacceptable to Gerald, whose impatience with Phil was by now evident to everyone in the family. He was in such a hurry for Phil to leave, in fact, that he did the apartment hunting himself. Ignoring his wife's protests, he began a campaign of expulsion, searching advertisements on craigslist.org until he found a suitable apartment. He devised a sort of provisional assisted living arrangement: two months' rent paid up front, a sixty-day, prepaid cell phone, and a two-month allowance— then the kicker, the directive to get a job immediately. The move took barely two hours. Phil packed his clothes, xbox 360, toiletries, and a few grocery items. His mother gave him the old sofa bed from the den and a kitchen set from a garage sale. At last Gerald was content: the nest was empty, and life could resume as planned.

The problem was the arrangement wasn't working out nearly so well for Phil. He was having a hard time finding a job, struggling with bus schedules to get him to interviews, and most of all, dissatisfied with living alone. Two months later, broke and depressed, he asked his parents if he could move back home. It took some convincing on the part of his mother and paternal uncle, and eventually Gerald gave in. After returning home, Phil started to attend family counseling with his parents. As the sessions progressed, Gerald came to learn about developmental differences in adolescents: how maturation and readiness to leave home vary according to a child's temperament. It took some time, but eventually Gerald began to understand that what his son needed, perhaps more than anything, was to be met at his actual developmental level. With support from his counselor and his uncle, Phil summoned the confidence to get a job. He tired quickly of riding the bus around Phoenix and, within a couple months, wanted to get his driver's license. He met a young lady and started taking her out on dates. He began to pay his parents $200 a month in rent, which they saved and returned to him when he found an apartment on his own, two years later. Phil was excited to be on his way.

For some young adults, developmental disabilities set the tone and pace of the separation and individuation process. Parents of adult children with special needs will see parallels in the dance of differentiation of their children, but their direct involvement, or that of other care providers, may last a lifetime. Should parents want a resource that addresses the young adult with special needs, they may wish to read Anne Ford's *On Their Own: Creating an Independent Future for Your Adult Child with Learning Disabilities and* ADHD.[1]

Your Child's Environment

Life, as we all know, seldom unfolds predictably: the pace at which a young adult achieves emancipation from his parents, both emotionally and proximally, is often shaped by unexpected life events that alter the timeline of a child's maturation. These events constitute the environment in which the dance of separation occurs. They can range from benign, positive occurrences—an opportunity for the entire family to live abroad for a year—to more serious circumstances, such as job loss and bankruptcy for parents, or death in the family. For the purposes of this book, we will focus on unwelcome events, which we'll examine now.

Death of a Parent. The loss of a parent, whether through accident, illness, suicide, or other means, can dramatically alter an adult child's path, influencing his decisions and ability to follow through with them. Quitting college, returning home to attend community college, postponing moving out of the family home—each may be a part of the child's response to death. How well the young person responds to loss often depends, among other things, on the circumstances of the surviving family members. If there are younger siblings at home, the adult child may be needed, for a time, to help care for her brothers or sisters. If the widowed parent is without a job, the child may feel compelled to provide financial support. Moving back home does not mean a person lacks the maturity to go forward; she may simply be setting aside her goals temporarily, to see that her family's needs are supported.

Out of deeply felt sympathy and love, children may feel an understandable need to console their surviving parents. Katherine was one such young woman. When her father died after a long battle with Lou Gehrig's disease, her mother, Martha, was not only grief-stricken, but emotionally and physically worn out. Katherine, just weeks away from leaving for college to pursue her dream of becoming an anthropologist, decided to delay enrollment. Her mother had dropped hint after hint about how pleased she was to have Katherine around (using the word "God-send"), and Katherine, sensitive to her mother's needs, felt uneasy even broaching the topic of leaving for school. When the enrollment window for the next semester came, Katherine decided to further postpone her acceptance and stay home. Hearing this, Katherine's mother cried with relief.

In this case, Martha's emotional dependency delayed her daughter's development. Extended family members who recognized the relationship was becoming unhealthy quietly voiced their concerns, but Martha was blind to the potential risks of her behavior, going so far as to brag she had found a new best friend. For Katherine, however, caring for her mother full-time meant deferring her dream of studying anthropology. She felt trapped and angry; worse, she felt guilty for having such thoughts. Katherine had done what she had thought was in her mother's best interest. Now it was time for Martha to consider her daughter's needs. She'd never been a particularly outgoing woman, and had relied on Katherine as her main social outlet. It was going to be a big leap for Martha to let go of her best friend, a move she was reluctant to make. Unfortunately, when I last encountered the family, Katherine was still living at home caring for her mother and the relationship had hardly changed.

We are probably safe in assuming that Martha wants what's best for her daughter, but her own grief—and lack of a sufficient social network—were interfering with her ability to let her daughter go. Were Martha to get additional help, be it through counseling, support groups, or social activities, she might have expressed a clearer message to Katherine that it is okay for her to resume her own life course. While a young adult's path may have its diversions, there is no reason she should give up her goals altogether. Finding a way forward for both parent and child is achievable and can yield benefits for both.

Serious Illness of a Parent. As with a death, a parent's serious illness can restrict an adolescent's ease of movement through the phases of separation and individuation. There can be grieving, not just in instances of death, but illness as well. But whereas a death is a finite event that allows the bereaved to begin working toward closure, a chronic illness does not. Depending on the severity of the illness, a young adult may have to cope with anticipatory grieving, or ongoing uncertainty about the well-being of her parent. Seventeen-year-old Raelynn's is a textbook case. An exceptionally bright and talented high school student, Raelynn had supportive and loving parents, whose marriage was full of joy. The biggest source of stress for the family was that both parents had chronic—though not life threatening—illnesses. Still, life carried on normally, until an opportunity presented itself to Raelynn during her senior year of high school. Through her school's music program, she had the chance to travel with her choir to perform at St. Olaf's College in Minnesota. For Raelynn, the thought of being out of contact with her parents (before cell phones had become ubiquitous) was nothing short of terrifying. This was a teenage girl, after all, who would wake up at least once during the night to check on her parents in their bedroom. Although it was important to Raelynn to make the trip, she knew it was going to be an uphill battle. The fear of separating from her parents when they were chronically unwell was virtually unbearable to her, and she was having second thoughts about making the trip at all.

Eventually, her parents took her to a therapist, and the two worked out a solution. Her father was a professional audiobook reader, and Raelynn would take one of his books with her, so she could listen to his voice when she began to feel lonely. The plan was a terrific success: Raelynn still had her homesick moments, but the five-day trip proved to be a big step forward for her and her parents. Even in difficult circumstances, a child must learn to be apart from their loved ones if she is to become independent. Raelynn demonstrated that while this may be hard, there are creative ways to take the needed steps to make this happen.

Divorce. Children of divorced parents often become very close to their parents and remain tightly connected throughout their lives. Due to financial constraints, some young adults continue living with their parents to share expenses. Generally, these arrangements are fine. But, if the parent becomes too close to the child, boundaries between the caregiver and child can blur, leading to a delay in the natural process of separation.

Adult children look to parents for guidance but also for signs as to how their parents are feeling. When things are amiss, children may postpone their quest for independence, particularly if they feel their parents will not be okay without having them nearby. Accustomed to exceptional closeness, children of divorce often feel anxious when pulling away from their parents. Differentiation may occur later than it does for children in the general population and is, at times, fraught with friction.

For some children, differentiation can mean coming to terms with a parent's new romantic partner. Larry is a young man who understands this well. His older sister moved out of the family's Detroit home when he was fourteen. Several years later—the same year she got married—his parents filed for divorce. Larry and his mother became very close. Finances were tight as Larry's father, who suffered recurring periods of unemployment, was unable to contribute much. To help fill the gap, Larry got an after-school job and began paying for more and more of his own necessities. He was so thrifty that he even managed to give his mother money for rent. In some ways, Larry showed all the signs of a mature young adult. He helped out with the rent, he took classes part-time at the local college, and he even offered to live at home after high school graduation.

All this was good news for the family financially, but his mother worried that Larry was missing out on his social life. It wasn't until his mother entered a serious relationship that Larry began to consider his own future, not because he was no longer worried about his mother, but because his mother and her new boyfriend made it clear they expected to have the house to themselves.

A few months later when his mother's boyfriend moved in, Larry felt hurt and rejected. In his mind, he was being replaced by someone who could not possibly love his mother as much as he did. But his protests went unheeded. It soon became clear the new boyfriend was not going anywhere soon. Larry could not stand the open affection his mother and her boyfriend showed to one another, and he withdrew to his room. His mother became aware that although she and her boyfriend had greater privacy, Larry had pretty much stopped talking to her. She made a point of letting him know how much she loved and appreciated all he had done for her, while conveying the idea that, like him, she also needed to have relationships with men and women her own age. She arranged to have a weekly lunch outing with Larry. She suggested dinners out with her and her boyfriend, eventually asking him if he wanted to bring a date.

As Larry became convinced his mother was not "abandoning" him, he felt more at ease hanging out with his friends. Now that his mother had come to understand the dynamics of the situation, she could take the necessary steps to affirm her need for her own private life. At the same time, she could demonstrate to Larry that her love for him would endure. Mother and son had finally discovered new boundaries that worked for them both.

Illness or Injury of the Child. Almost without fail, a serious childhood illness will affect a young person's emancipation, which is why I try to pay close attention to outstanding factors in the person's life, such as major surgeries, accidents, or illnesses, when gathering information from clients. Unfortunately, the pathway to independence can be especially challenging for children with serious illness, and parents may struggle when the time comes to expect mature, adult-like behavior. While some may criticize a parent for doing too much for her child, the decision is often based on the child's history, defined, in many cases, by the child's specialized needs.

To illustrate how all this may affect the separation and individuation process, consider the case of Nancy, a happily married, licensed practical nurse and the mother of nine-year-old Bethany. Like many children her age, Bethany was active and curious about life. Away at summer camp in northern Wisconsin, Bethany was out for a run when her foot got caught in a pothole in the long driveway near one of the cabins. As she fell to the ground, her leg twisted and snapped. What at first appeared to be a simple fracture turned out to be a compound one, requiring several surgeries, months in a wheelchair, and a delayed start to her school year. Nancy quit her job to stay home with Bethany and help with the physical therapy. Nancy did her new job well. She was there to take care of her daughter's needs, and the two became extraordinarily close.

Now fast forward to the teen and early adult years: Bethany is still very close to her mother, but not very adventurous. Worried her daughter will "overdo it" with any kind of physical activity, Nancy dissuades her from being more active. But this strategy only works for so long. Soon Nancy's constant warnings begin to sound preachy and overbearing, and despite her mother's repeated advice to the contrary, Bethany takes up hiking with her friends. As her mother's protests intensify, Bethany grows to resent her mother's interference in her life. Eventually, she stops obeying her mother's requests altogether. Nancy, for her part, sees her daughter as ignoring the reality of a physical limitation. But the more she warns Bethany of the risks of hiking on a weak leg, the more reckless Bethany becomes. At one point she even signs up for a half marathon in Seattle, making the case she is in fine shape to run the race, and if she's not, well, she'll pop a pain pill. "Get a life and stay out of mine," she tells her mother spitefully.

Unsure of what to do, Nancy seeks counseling. To her surprise, the therapist tells her what is happening is perfectly healthy. "How," Nancy asks in amazement, "could that possibly be?" The therapist explains that Bethany's need to differentiate from her mother is the main developmental task at hand, that Bethany's need to emancipate from her mother is a natural part of the maturation process and that her compulsion to do so is very strong at this stage of her life, stronger, even, than common sense. She advises Nancy to back off and let her daughter make her own decision as to how she is going to care for herself. "What if she gets hurt again?" Nancy asks. "That is always a possibility," the therapist replies matter-of-factly. Only through additional sessions does Nancy come to understand that, however nerve-wracking it may be, Bethany has to have the opportunity to stand on her own and experience the consequences of her actions in order to grow.

A child's illness need not be physical to be debilitating. Many parents have to cope with adult children who have been diagnosed with a mental illness. While in some situations, the illness has been evident for years, sometimes symptoms do not emerge until the child's mid-teenage years or early adulthood. Bipolar disorder and schizophrenia are among those that can blindside both the parent and the child. The extent of the impact on the individual and family varies, but parents are often called upon to extend the amount of time devoted to active parenting. In the case of severe mental illness, working with your therapist or in conjunction with your adult child's is frequently a must, along with having outside supports. One such group is NAMI, the National Alliance on Mental Illness. NAMI, with chapters across the country, provides programs and services for people whose lives have been touched by serious mental illness.

Substance Abuse and Addiction. Using drugs or alcohol constitutes a decision on a person's part, but the easy availability of such substances is part of the environment in which adolescents grow up. A young person may experiment with drugs or alcohol for any number of reasons: pressure to be a part of a group, curiosity, boredom, defiance or rebellion. Whatever the reason, for too many young people, that initial experimentation eventually leads to patterns of behavior that shape the emancipation process in unsavory ways.

The result is that rather than spending his time and energy in his self- and interpersonal development through work, school or training programs and social activities, the drug-involved young adult's healthy growth becomes derailed. A commonly held belief in the field of addictions is that a person's emotional development becomes arrested at the age at which his focus turns to his drug of choice. Thus, you may see a twenty-five or thirty year-old man who behaves more like he is fifteen.

Some substance use results in glaring behavior—the young man coming home high on methamphetamines or falling-down drunk. But more subtle is the slow erosion of responsible behavior on the part of chronic pot users. Take Marshall, for example. His parents sought therapy out of frustration, because, while their older adult daughter seemed to claim her independence on a reasonable schedule, Marshall did not. He dropped out of high school during his junior year and took up permanent residence in his bedroom. His parents knew he had smoked marijuana since his freshman year, but they turned a blind eye to it since his father had experimented with drugs himself as a teen.

Marshall was twenty-two by the time his parents went to counseling. He was still making faithless promises to contact the local community college about getting his GED. Since he was such an amiable guy and helped out around the house, his parents didn't really mind his being there. They knew he still "smoked a little dope," but did not prohibit him from doing so. His dad, however, was increasingly frustrated because, GED preparation aside, Marshall did not work. He'd had a short stint as a courtesy clerk at Safeway, which ended because he just couldn't make it to work. Marshall's parents worked all day and it was infuriating for them to come home and find Marshall starting his day at dinner time. Each day he'd leave for a few hours, come home smelling like pot, and retreat to his room, where he had a small TV and a computer. As the months dragged on, Marshall's list of excuses just got longer: the economy was bad; he had no "wheels" to get a job; there was no way he'd flip burgers and be laughed at by his friends; he felt tired. His parents offered to drive him to interviews, help with his applications. They even talked to their friends about finding Marshall work. He took the occasional odd job, helping someone chop wood or rake leaves, but that was it. But because his mother couldn't stand the thought of her son on the street, their threats to put him out always stopped short of any real action.

The therapist worked with Marshall's parents to help them get some perspective on the situation. He spoke about the separation and individuation process, noting that Marshall seemed to be stuck and was probably addicted to marijuana. The therapist made the assumption, presumably correct, that, short of major changes, Marshall's behavior could go on for years. Together with the therapist, Marshall's parents devised a plan to invite their son to a session, not to ambush him, but to have a talk in a neutral setting about how the entire family seemed rather stuck. The parents didn't like the people they were becoming with their son, and he certainly didn't relish their nagging. When Marshall reluctantly attended the session, he was surprised to discover that the therapist was interested in his perspective. Marshall admitted he just didn't know what to do and, in fact, was scared to do anything. He agreed that he might have a problem with marijuana, and that, quite frankly, he had avoided looking for a job for fear of having to take a drug test. He agreed to get a drug evaluation as a condition of continuing to live at home, and his parents agreed to stop badgering him. After the results of the evaluation, they would all meet again to consider the next steps. The situation was by no means resolved, but Marshall and his parents felt hope for the first time in a long while.

Any of these environmental factors, as well as the child's temperament, can make the separation and individuation process a bumpy and, at times, painful period in a family's life. Parents often ask me how much help to give their children, and when and if to raise or lower expectations. Here are some points to consider in making that decision:

1. *Pay attention to cues from your child.*

Has she consistently preferred your company to that of her peers? Is she reluctant to get a driver's license or go to school functions? Does she prefer the company of people much younger than her? Does she talk about not looking forward to growing up, or sabotage her own efforts at getting a job? All these may be clues that the young person is not quite ready to move into life's adult phase. In the case of severe dysfunction, the questions become even more serious. Is your daughter emotionally or physically abusive to you? Are you afraid of her? Is she abusing substances? As long as someone is actively abusing substances, her self-awareness will be limited. A number of experts in the field of addiction claim that an addict's emotional development is arrested at the age at which they began using.

2. *Recognize that environmental stressors impact the developmental process.*

Do not get hung up with guilt. Every day people get divorced, die, get sick, and lose their jobs. If we have learned nothing else by middle age, hopefully we've at least learned that we don't have total control in our lives or those of our children. Identify the stressors and assess their impact. Get appropriate help.

Remember, unplanned events and even crises can build character and resilience in our children. It is not the "easy A" your son got in English that he'll recall with pride in his later years. More likely it will be the hard-won "B" from another teacher or managing a job and a full-time class load simultaneously to attain his dream of completing his college degree.

3. *Take care of your own issues.*

The task of separation and individuation, while a natural part of everyone's life, is difficult enough on its own merit. Do not give your adult child more reasons to avoid this process. Look at yourself. Are you giving direct or subtle messages to your daughter that you are unable to take care of your own needs? If so, you may be inadvertently undermining her attempts at attaining appropriate distance from you. If you are lonely, depressed, or otherwise having a hard time, seek help through friends, family, or professionals. Your daughter should not have to feel guilty for pursuing her life. Have you been such a best friend to your daughter that she has not developed significant friendships among peers her own age? Encourage her to transfer some of her loyalty to her peer group. Consider declining her next shopping invitation and suggesting she take a friend from work. If you get jealous at the idea of her having friends other than yourself, then this is an area where you need some work.

4. *Resist the urge to make everything easy for your child.*

Your daughter will never develop the necessary skills for navigating adulthood if you make things too easy for her. The accomplished guitarist only becomes so after years of practice. In the process, she develops calluses on her fingertips, which prepare her to spend long hours practicing and performing. An analogous situation occurs in parenting. By making things too easy for our adult children, we prevent them from developing experiential "calluses." Before your adult child moves out, challenge her to live within a budget. She may resist your efforts simply because you are suggesting something new and out of her comfort zone. But do not let her discomfort stop you from doing what ultimately will become a valuable lesson. Some struggles make us stronger.

PART THREE

Making Things Better: Real People,
Real Problems, Real Solutions

CHAPTER EIGHT

"Those Aren't My Values"

Substance Abuse and Severe Behavior Problems

Sometimes parents have an adult child whose values directly oppose their own. You should expect your child to reject at least some parental ideals during adolescence when teens often define themselves as what their parents are *not*. This is the necessary developmental process of "separation and individuation," in which a child will test parental values in order to develop autonomous views and opinions.

Friction between a parent and child's beliefs only becomes a matter of concern when it extends beyond the adolescent years. Even then, most unconventional adult lifestyle choices usually do not pose a threat to the grown child's ability to function as an adult. Such attitudes do become problematic, however, when they lead the child to a pattern of alcohol and drug abuse, or criminal activity. There is no way for you as a parent to prepare for a lifestyle that puts you in a position to bail out your thirty-one-year-old daughter from jail, get a restraining order against your son, take custody of your grandchildren, or watch your child self-destruct. Nevertheless, if your child is tumbling down that path, there are some proactive ways to protect yourself and your family.

Parents of destructive adult children often carry the invisible burdens of guilt, shame, anger, and sadness. They feel they have failed in their most basic duty: raising a child to become a functional adult. It is not easy to remain hopeful when the child for whom they had high hopes is bent on self-destruction. While others at work may bemoan long hours, afflicted parents frequently welcome the stability and consistency of the work day as a chance to shed their emotional weight. Leaving work means heaving the load onto their backs once more and trudging into the land of self-recrimination and unpredictability. Although they usually do not broadcast their efforts, these parents may expend incredible sums of money and significant emotional resources attempting to help their children.

Whether afflicted parents choose to stand by a child unfailingly or separate from the child for their own self-preservation, they often make the choice that is right for their family. As a testament to both human vulnerability and strength, parents of wayward children, time and again, channel their suffering into forging new and productive paths in their lives—they don't want to be pitied or condemned, but understood.

Zoe and Ray

Zoe, a witty and warm divorcee, was in her fifties when she met Ray. She quickly bonded with his two daughters and three grandchildren, and, marrying Ray, she welcomed her new role as stepmother and step-grandmother. One of Ray's daughters functioned well, but the other—Sarah—had a history of escalating drug and substance use that began after she was raped at age thirteen. Zoe was concerned but not demoralized. A licensed therapist in her third decade of recovery from alcohol dependence, she considered herself well equipped to offer Sarah support in overcoming her emotional trauma and dangerous addictions.

Shortly before Zoe met her, Sarah had a promising career and earned a six-figure income. However, after her marriage to an abusive husband ended in divorce, Sarah's substance use intensified and compromised her ability to function. Sarah's addictions left her in no position to offer her teenage son any boundaries or guidance, and the boy began to develop difficulties of his own. His misbehavior escalated to the point that he dropped out of school and, as Zoe strongly suspected, began using drugs himself.

Zoe and Ray actively supported Sarah's attempts at sobriety, even paying for treatment multiple times. At one point they helped Sarah enter a detox program at an inpatient facility for women. For months they supported Sarah and attended the facility's family classes, hopeful that recovery was imminent. However they were disheartened when Sarah openly denied any alcohol abuse, for they knew that wasn't true. Zoe confronted Sarah, who held firm to her conviction that she no longer had a drinking problem. But she did have a problem, and only a few weeks after leaving the program, she fell back into dangerous drinking habits, including driving while drunk.

It took some time, but Sarah eventually admitted to having a problem and entered another inpatient program. With this encouraging step, Zoe and Ray once again allowed themselves to hope for Sarah's recovery. Still, Sarah was far from cooperative. Despite voluntarily seeking treatment, she did not take any of the program suggestions seriously and often complained about her inpatient treatment counselors. Zoe's experiences allowed her to understand that Sarah would not begin the process of recovery as long as she continued to focus her complaints on other people. "You're here to focus on you, not on your counselors," she told Sarah one night over dinner. But the advice fell on deaf ears. Sarah would not submit to the treatment and continued to abuse alcohol and drugs after leaving the facility.

Zoe and Ray retired several years ago and now live eighteen hundred miles from Sarah. They try to keep in touch, but Sarah seems determined to shut them out and has not answered their calls or e-mails for months. They will periodically hear news of Sarah's activity through a concerned ex-boyfriend, also upset by Sarah's self-destructive substance abuse, who has decided to break off his relationship with her because of her addiction. As one young man, Nicolas, put it, he could no longer watch her "lie on the basement floor and puke her guts out." The last time Zoe and Ray heard from Nicolas, he predicted, sadly, that Sarah would be homeless by the end of the month.

Zoe's Observations

Zoe sees parallels between her own struggle with alcohol dependence and her stepdaughter's ongoing substance abuse. But long ago Zoe made the definitive choice that Sarah still evades: To stop using.

As both a former alcoholic and chemical dependency coun-selor, Zoe seems to have the ideal background to help someone like Sarah. Still, she wonders at times if she adopted the right approach: "Maybe I'd feel better if I'd been more of a therapist than a mom. If I had it to do over, I would have confronted her more. I didn't speak up when I could have." But she did, and so did many people: Ray, Sarah's boyfriends, and other family members. Sarah simply chose not to listen.

Rather than fight the losing battle of trying to force Sarah to lis-ten, Zoe has chosen to focus her efforts on being a supportive wife. She introduced Ray to the advice of Al-Anon, a support group for the friends and family members of problem drinkers, to "detach with love." With Zoe's help, Ray has come to recognize the limits of his own control and realize that enabling Sarah will not help her overcome her drinking problem.

Zoe and Ray are well aware of Sarah's manipulative attempts to convince her father of his complicity in her drinking. In their last phone conversation, Sarah exclaimed, "You were such a shitty dad, so why should I be any different?" Rather than allowing himself to be personally insulted by the accusations, Ray has stepped back and attempted to view the situation objectively. He is not a bad parent; to the contrary, he has taken an active role in Sarah's upbringing and has supported her attempts at recovery. With Zoe's help Ray has been able to look past Sarah's hurtful accusations and understand the three "Cs" from Al-Anon: "You didn't *cause* it; you can't *control* it; you can't *cure* it." Ray doesn't just espouse these words. He has, in the words of Al-Anon, "integrated them into his being."

Despite this grim assessment, Zoe offers some reassuring words for other parents: "Take care of yourself. You will have more hope if you refuse to enable your children than if you spend time on what does not work. You have to learn through your own personal experiences . . . We don't know what 'the bottom' [for an adult child] will be." If Sarah wanted to live with them, what would Zoe say? "She would have to be involved in a treatment program and have proof of sobriety before coming to stay with us. Absolutely no drugs or alcohol, or she'd have to leave immediately." Would they give her money? "No, it would go to drugs." How about co-signing for a loan? "No way; that's been done in the past."

My Observations

Zoe and Ray could have chosen to erode their retirement savings and compromise their physical and mental health to try to rescue Sarah from her addiction, but her behavior almost undoubtedly would have continued. They could have isolated themselves from others as penance for Sarah's poor choices and lack of self-discipline, but, again, Sarah's behavior almost certainly would have gone on just as before.

Wisely, they have chosen a saner path. They remain engaged with the rest of their family and enjoy watching their grandchildren grow up. They stay active in their community, volunteering at a handful of local organizations. Zoe works with college students, who are drawn to her for comfort and advice. She is often saddened by the fact that so many young people consider her a "second mom" while Sarah—her own stepdaughter—still rebuffs her attempts to help. Still, the work is rewarding.

The grief caused by a child's addiction will never disappear completely, but parents should not let the pain consume their lives. Talking frankly about her daughter did cause Zoe a great deal of anguish during our interview, and it is important to understand that periodic moments of grief are a necessary part of the healing process. Like Zoe and Ray, all parents owe it to themselves and their loved ones to move on when their child's manipulation endangers their health, work, and emotional stability. Not all situations, however, have such painful outcomes. For a more uplifting perspective, let's turn to the story of Ursula and her son, Allen.

Ursula and Allen

Ursula and her husband, Lance, live in the Midwest, and both have rewarding careers—Ursula as a tenured history professor, and Lance as an engineer. They are the dedicated Christian parents of two adult children. Their daughter, Chrissa, who was a polite, respectful child is now a middle school teacher training to be a school administrator. Their son, Allen, however, was a rebellious young man who caused his parents trouble from a very early age. Ursula describes Allen as "too everything," a highly active, emotional, and intelligent man whose inordinately reactive behavior as a child puzzled every doctor Ursula and Lance sought for guidance. Although diagnosis proved elusive, Ursula and Lance did learn from the doctors they visited that such reactivity in young children can lead to attempts to self-medicate. Allen was no exception. In high school, he fell into a pattern of alcohol use that resulted in a six-week psychiatric hospitalization. While there, psychiatrists prescribed medication intended to help with Allen's addiction. Ursula thought the medication was useful, but Allen disliked taking the pills and eventually stopped.

Despite what Ursula felt was, on her part, adequate support, Allen's erratic behavior escalated and twice earned him six-month sentences in the county jail for alcohol-related offenses. In the second and more serious of the two incidents, Allen and his live-in girlfriend, Kira, were arguing in a tavern. Both were literally "falling-down drunk." In the heat of the dispute, Kira fell off her bar stool and hit the floor. Allen told her to stay there, for fear he'd drop her if she tried to get up. "I don't want to hurt you, so stay down on the floor!" he cried. Another patron heard him, and thinking the comment a threat, called the police. In the wake of the September 11 attacks, anything that sounded like a threat was viewed as a terrorist act. Allen was charged with three felonies, and Ursula was so devastated she became physically ill: "I immediately took to my bed; I couldn't even stand up." On a reduced charge, Allen was sentenced to six months in jail. In order to cope, Ursula went into therapy.

Due to concerns he was a terrorist, Allen was forbidden while incarcerated to take part in AA meetings or get counseling for himself. He was, however, allowed to attend religious services and came to embrace Christianity. Allen's improved behavior stood out, and he eventually became a crew chief in jail. Ursula visited him weekly and took his young daughters to see him twice a month. Lance and their daughter were critical of Ursula's actions.

To them, she was just an enabler, but Ursula thinks otherwise: "Our son hit bottom early. I saw families whose kids had gone through the [AA] program five or six times. I didn't have their kind of experience. I didn't have the scar tissue build-up as they did, where they'd say 'here we go again.' Don't tell me that I enabled him." She recalls that Allen was released from jail at ten o' clock at night with no shoes and no money, left in a remote area outside of town, and warned to be gone from the property in an hour or he'd be returned to his cell. It was hardly a way to get off to a decent start. "What would he have done if I had not been there to help him?" she wonders.

Allen's eventual release was contingent upon his going into rehab for six months. Through his mother's dedicated appeal, Allen was accepted into a six-month residential program run by the Salvation Army. During that period, he learned to live substance-free, developed skills for coping with his emotions, and strengthened his spiritual beliefs. While he was in the treatment facility, Ursula regularly participated in the family program. She says that although the family has helped their son financially, she expects him to pay them back.

And for the most part, Allen has done so. Since his release and rehabilitation, he has held various part-time jobs, and now holds a stable job as a restaurant manager. At one point he was even working two jobs at once in order to reduce his debts. In the three years since his release, he has returned to the jail each week to give testimonials to Narcotics Anonymous and AA groups.

Several years ago Ursula and Lance moved into a new home large enough to accommodate Allen and his daughters, who come to visit nearly every other weekend. Eight years after his release, Allen appears to have reclaimed his life. In addition to his job in a high-end restaurant, he has become more involved in his church. He is married, as well, and recently bought a new home for his blended family. Ursula, for her part, loves being a closely involved grandmother.

Ursula's Observations

Ursula believes her parents were poor examples of how to raise a child. She shares the story of how, at age eight, she had her appendix removed and became quite sick in the hospital. Her mother was visiting a relative in another city and did not arrive to see Ursula until midway through the operation. Things did not improve when once she made it to the hospital. Standing at the foot of the bed, she fainted almost instantaneously, "taking all the attention to herself," Ursula claims. Her mother was escorted out of the room and did not return until long after the operation. To Ursula, the story illustrates what it is like to have parents who turn away when their children need them the most.

Thankfully, Ursula did have wonderful grandparents, whom she credits with raising her. As a young child, she often turned down evening television at home to go next door to her grandparent's house, where they'd sit, talk, and listen to the radio—leading a life far less chaotic than that of Ursula's parents. Her grandmother, who had raised twelve children, embodied the qualities Ursula admires to this day: love, a sense of humor, spiritual values, and hard work.

Ursula wants to pass on her grandmother's gifts to Allen and Chrissa. Rather than refusing to help her children as her own parents had, she has embraced every opportunity to do so. Still, she understands the perils of going too far in the other direction. For a long time, she tried too hard to be perfect. Now that her children are adults, she realizes that perfection is not necessary. It's okay to be "good enough."

Ursula and Allen have talked about the nature of the assistance she provided him when he was in need. Allen says she *did* enable him, but Ursula disagrees. People who are depressed, she argues, can't take the first couple steps on their own. "I wasn't being an enabler. I was being supportive." She felt alone in her advocacy for Allen for a long time. Eventually her husband and daughter apologized to her, saying they were wrong. "Sometimes," Ursula concludes, "we just have to be patient and wait."

My Observations

Many parents have adult children who have gone through the cycle of addiction and treatment multiple times. The emotional scars these parents may develop as a result have the same effect as physical ones. They provide an additional layer of protective scar tissue as it were so the wound can heal. That partial loss of feeling, though difficult to accept, allows for healthy detachment. In this case, there was a benefit to Allen's hitting "rock bottom" so early in life: Ursula's energy to help her son had not burnt out. She had the strength to support her son even without the rest of her family's support. What looked like enabling to Lance and Chrissa turned out to be the right amount of help for Allen. The timing was right for him to grasp the "branch" that was extended to him in the form of a treatment program through the Salvation Army.

Lessons Learned

Trouble with adult children does not arise spontaneously. Many parents with difficult adult children have noted problems since childhood. It is easy for parents to blame themselves for a child's delinquency or addiction, despite their having other children who are very functional adults and show no signs of substance abuse. Be careful of getting sucked into an abusive relationship. Parents who internalize the blame for an adult child's poor lifestyle choices can become physically ill or emotionally distraught, as we saw with Ursula and Zoe. The more a parent internalizes blame the more likely she is to become depressed and isolated, which will affect not only her but the other members of her family. The fact is that intense parenting challenges can "derail" even the most grounded among us. It is best to do what Ursula and Zoe did: seek help—be it through counseling, friends, family, or your spiritual belief system.

If you have a child whose lifestyle is compromising her ability to function as a responsible adult, here are a few reminders to help you understand your role in the situation and the areas in which you are in control:

1. If someone becomes drug-involved, even the most effective parents can feel quite helpless. Seeking additional support for the child such as an inpatient treatment program may be an important first step toward recovery.

2. Most difficult young adults have a pattern of behavior that extends back to their childhood and teenaged years. Understanding this history can lend valuable clues about the origins of the child's substance abuse problem.

3. You get to decide how involved you should be in your child's problems. No one can or should decide what you should do.

4. Consider the impact of your child's behavior on the rest of the family. Other family members who are not acting out or showing obvious symptoms are likely suffering along with you.

5. Be clear on your values and the standards you set for your home. Sticking to these and requiring others living in the home to do likewise makes a firm, convincing statement and leaves you feeling empowered.

6. Manipulative young adults know that parents are prone to feeling guilt. Resist taking the blame for your child's behavior or predicament. Mature adults take responsibility for their own actions.

7. A time often comes when the parent has to withdraw in order to preserve her physical and mental health. Only you know when that time is.

- - - - - - - - - - - - - - - -

CHAPTER NINE

"She Just Won't Grow Up"

Slow to Bloom or Just Irresponsible?

When our children are young, there are times when we wish they'd stay that way forever: cute, cuddly, needing us as much as we need them. We cannot imagine a time when they are not in the house and under our care. Fast-forward one or two decades and our perspective shifts. Yes, we still want and need a relationship with them, but we know in our bones that to be truly independent, they must move on and assume the responsibilities of adulthood.

The eventuality of this separation is universal, but family customs and cultures dictate how, where, and when it happens. An American living in Queretaro, Mexico, just north of Mexico City, told me she heard the following from a native Mexican: "In the United States, adult children move out unless there is some specific reason to stay. In Mexico, they stay home unless there is some specific reason to leave." While this pattern may be customary in some cultures, the pervading American expectation is for young adults who have graduated from high school and college to be on their own within a few years.

Whether a young adult is living at home or elsewhere, parents will know when she has crossed the threshold into adulthood. Paying for one's own transportation and associated insurance, not asking parents for money to cover basic living expenses, treating parents with the same respect one desires for herself—these are all signs of maturation. The transition usually includes living independently, but that does not have to be the case. Many adult children and their parents can effectively live under the same roof in relative sanity (see chapter seventeen for a full discussion of how to make this work).

For example, unemployment as a result of a depressed economy may require a young man to return home to live while completing school, saving money, or transitioning between jobs. Usually this is temporary, a stop-gap measure while the young adult is preparing for the financial realities that come with independence.

The truly "adult" child living at home will have discussed expectations with his parents for residing there prior to moving in. He doesn't approach living at home as an entitlement, nor as a flophouse where he can come and go as he pleases. He may not have the funds to pay rent, but he should be able and willing to contribute to the household in other ways. I've known young adults who take on household duties or car maintenance. They also house-sit and care for pets while parents travel or they assist with the family business. The situation won't be perfect, but it can work.

Some young people, content to subsist on their parents' paychecks or unskilled part-time jobs, are hesitant to accept the responsibilities that come with adulthood. When that happens, parents face the daunting challenge of inspiring their young adult to move out of the nest. That is a tricky proposition, and timing is critical. You'll remember the example of Phil from chapter seven. When his parents pushed him to leave the safety of their home prematurely, the eviction backfired and he soon returned with his ego and confidence diminished. After the opportunity to mature another two years, he was ready for the next step in his development. In cases like these, young people usually give clues along the way that they are taking a little longer to blossom. They may avoid learning to drive, prefer the company of parents and siblings to friends, and even make direct statements that they don't want to grow up. Parents should resist the urge to make snap judgments about the cause for a child's reluctance to embrace adulthood. People are complex, and similar behavior can be the result of very different factors, many of them legitimate.

Often grown children express a desire for adulthood, but sabotage their own efforts at achieving it. Parents are torn—unsure whether to push harder and raise expectations, or back off and accept that they may harbor unrealistic notions of who their children will become. The following two examples are situations in which baby boomer mothers were challenged with adult children who, on the surface, didn't want to be adults. We will learn from their travails that, despite the difficulties of raising reluctant adults, the endeavor can be deeply rewarding. By setting appropriate expectations and boundaries, the two mothers profiled below came up with effective ways to maintain their integrity, while nudging their children in the right direction.

Melody

When forty-one-year-old Melody was nineteen she found out she was pregnant. As her family expected, she moved into her own apartment and became self-sufficient. Melody never regretted the decision to have her daughter Janna, but being an independent, young single mother was a constant struggle. Balancing a full-time job with the demands of bringing up her daughter required incredible energy, not to mention unrelenting commitment and sacrifice. While raising Janna, she took many opportunities to explain the consequences of her early pregnancy, hoping her daughter would make different decisions than she had made. They'd talked about both abstinence and birth control, and Janna gave her mother the impression she wouldn't have unprotected sex. But when Janna turned nineteen, having just graduated from high school and enrolled in community college, family history repeated itself: Janna got pregnant. Five months later, when she told her mother about the pregnancy, they both broke down.

As it happens, Melody rents out rooms to college students to supplement her income. Rather than have what she knew would be an emotional conversation in their crowded home, she drove Janna to a hotel and reserved a room so they could talk privately. Melody insisted her daughter write a list of pros and cons about carrying out the pregnancy, but Janna had already decided to have and keep the baby. Making a list was not going to change her mind. After many tearful nights of soul-searching, Melody accepted her daughter's decision and began to take steps to let go of her anxiety about the pregnancy. Recognizing Janna's choice was her own, she said to herself, "It's not my life. It's not about me. Let go of it. I'll just be the best grandmother I can be."

Janna had her baby and continued to live with her mother in the crowded rental property. She did not have a job. In the weeks that followed, the disrespect she'd shown her mother since her junior year in high school intensified, as did her demands. She did not hesitate to ask her mother for money to pay for gas, food, and incidentals; she felt entitled to it. But when Melody requested that her daughter share in the household duties, such as vacuuming and dish washing, Janna refused. She even protested when asked to take the trash to the curb for collection, saying she would carry the garbage as far as the trash can and be done with it. As the arguments intensified, Melody's stress level climbed steadily higher. Now it seemed as though the slightest provocation would set Janna off.

Something had to be done. Melody had already established stricter household rules, to lower the escalating tension and increase cooperation between herself and Janna. Though one such rule limited the number of times a friend could spend the night in a week, the baby's father and Janna's boyfriend, Jason, frequently exceeded his quota. A tipping point was reached when Jason came to retrieve his jacket after a lengthy stay. To communicate the seriousness of her intentions, Melody would not let him in the front door. Janna stormed out of the house screaming, her baby in her arms and Jason trailing after her. For more than a week, there was not a word from Janna. Just when she was losing hope, Melody received a phone call: "I still live there, don't I?" Janna asked. "We need to talk," replied her mother.

Melody had given the situation a great deal of thought. She feared not being able to see her grandson, to whom she had become strongly attached. But as she told herself, "I can't let that cloud my decision-making. I value myself too much." She was fed up with the battles and disrespect, and resolved to prohibit her daughter from living in the household until the tenor of their relationship changed. Her daughter's demands and behavior would not hold her hostage.

Melody's Observations

Melody is now adopting a new perspective, emboldened by her therapy and the reassurance of a leadership group in which she regularly participates. She has stopped using "you" statements, and she thinks about what she wants to say and how she wants to be heard. She "centers" herself and speaks slowly in an upright posture. "It's not about who is winning," she says. "By not allowing myself to be held hostage, each one of us can get what we want. Each of us has to give some, but I need to be respected for the rules that I do have."

Melody no longer quibbles over whether her daughter does enough housework because the argument is unproductive. Although she is well aware that Janna is driving on a suspended driver's license, that is another battle she's been willing to abandon. In her words: "That's her, not me. She has her own car. She's an adult. It will be up to her to figure it out if she gets stopped." Finally, Melody no longer hands out money freely to her daughter. When Janna asks, she says "no" without feeling guilty.

As for helping in the parenting role with her grandchild, Melody tries not to intervene. She leaves the parenting as much as possible to Janna, and has learned to respect Janna's perspective. Not long ago, she helped pay for a trip for Janna and her child to visit family in Guatemala. She hopes that seeing the less developed conditions of the rural town they visit will encourage Janna's appreciation of the comfort of her life in the United States.

Melody continues to rent out rooms in her home to college students to supplement her income. Some of the young people have become like family to her, returning year after year, and although she fears that Janna resents her closeness with the boarders, this does not stop her. She plans to continue renting rooms for her own personal and professional growth.

My Observations

Melody's experiences show that it is often through crises that we show rejuvenating growth. Stronger than ever before, Melody has learned that no matter how much she tries to set limits on Janna's behavior, her daughter may refuse to listen. She and Janna are in the early stages of the dance of differentiation. Janna claims to want to be treated as an adult, but her behaviors indicate she is still resisting the responsibilities that come with this role. Giving birth to a child, while introducing new caregiving demands, has not propelled her into maturity as it can for some children.

Melody's own mother, who never expected to have her child's baby in her home, made it clear to her daughter that she had to figure things out on her own. Janna has never had that kind of pressure. As long as her mother continued to give her money, she had no incentive to move toward independence. Cutting back on Janna's monthly allowance should be seen as a move of prudence on Melody's part, despite Janna's obvious displeasure. By doing so, Melody is not only helping her daughter but freeing herself from what could be years of enabling.

Melody took a risk. Her mental and physical health were at stake, and she needed a way to regain control of her home. She found authority by becoming very deliberate in her actions, giving careful consideration to her voice and body language, as well as the content of her communications with Janna. At the same time she has remained focused on her career, not allowing herself to become so embroiled in the maturation process of her daughter that she loses sight of her own ambitions.

Norma

Norma and her second husband, Nate, have been together for fourteen years. Nate, who has no biological children, came into the lives of Norma and her son Seth when the boy was eight years old. Nate welcomed the role of stepfather, and Seth quickly warmed to him. The arrangement worked well until not long after the wedding, when Seth's biological father heard his son use the word "Dad" in reference to Nate. Taking this as a personal affront, he chastised his son and made a point of reminding him, "*Nate* is not your father. *I* am." The consequences of this exchange were further reaching than Norma had imagined. Not only did Seth stop referring to Nate as his father, but, in the wake of this rejection, Nate retreated from the fatherly role. From Norma's point of view, this was an unfortunate turn of events. In her assessment, Seth's biological father did not behave as a father should. He treated Seth more like a peer, often speaking to his son about his girlfriends disrespectfully, referring to them as "bitches" and other chauvinist slurs.

After high school Seth enrolled in a technical college program for computer-aided drafting. He took out two loans to pay for school, but learned within the first several months that the field was not right for him. He stopped attending classes and was ultimately suspended from the program. When it came time to start repaying the loans, he failed to do so. With a damaged credit rating, twenty-year-old Seth could not qualify for a lease on an apartment and was relegated to living at home.

The delayed pace of Seth's progression towards maturity was a consistent source of stress for Norma. At his age, she was on her own building a successful interior design business. She had expected her children to follow that same trajectory, and her challenge, she now understands, is to see Seth as the person who he is, not the person she thinks he should be. After leaving college, Seth sought employment so that he could begin paying off his loans. He started out slowly, working in a furniture warehouse part time. Eventually, he became a full-time employee with benefits. As he was getting his "sea legs," he began to form a new circle of friends.

Norma and Nate allowed Seth to live at home while he was working and repaying his loans, with the understanding that when asked he would help with household chores and yard maintenance. His greatest challenge was his habit of putting off payments to creditors. Norma gave him verbal reminders, which she called "nudges" but Seth viewed as nagging. Still, despite their disputes over Seth's loan repayment, Norma believes her son was beginning to realize her motive was not to harass him but to prepare him to live on his own.

With time Seth started to manage a full-time job and pay his bills ahead of schedule. Norma and Nate increased their financial expectations of him. He began to pay rent, buy his own food, and take responsibility for his car insurance payments. In one of the final steps toward Seth's independence, Norma and Nate transferred the car title to his name, giving him complete accountability for his own transportation needs. Now, two years after my first interview with Norma, Seth is entirely independent. He lives in his own apartment and covers his expenses. He has advanced far enough in his career that he is able to make ends meet without having to get a second job or ask his parents for money. Norma has moved to a more hands-off approach to parenting: seeing her son weekly and communicating more frequently by text message and e-mail. Despite a few wrinkles, Norma is pleased with Seth's progress and enjoys her now-empty nest.

While Norma and Nate have supported one another in their parenting, they've at times held divergent opinions about what is best for Seth. In Norma's mind, Nate's lack of a biological child has kept him from fully understanding her point of view. "When I married Nate, I was choosing a mate, as well as a dad for Seth." While she did get both, she believes Nate has been unable to feel the "anguish" of parenting that she has experienced. Nevertheless, she is grateful for his involvement. His example has taught Seth honesty, integrity, and a respect for women. And it was Nate, after all, who believed Seth to be a "capable adult man," long before Norma came to view him this way. His model of parenting has taught Norma to give Seth more room and avoid being his fallback option every time he is broke or in distress.

Norma believes that embracing Nate's hands-off approach to parenting is the only way for her son to be emotionally and financially prepared to be on his own. But she will not abandon her son. As she says, "there is no way on God's green earth that I could not have a home for my son if he needed it."

Norma's Observations

Norma sees her parenting as unconditional love, not enabling. Enabling, she says, is doing something for someone that he can do for himself. She believes her reminders and nudges were necessary for Seth, though she recognizes the need to maintain healthy boundaries: "This is just a journey with no end. Acceptance is the key . . . who your child is, who you are. Once you reach the top of a hurdle, there will be another."

In her own life, Norma experienced periods of struggle, including a divorce from her first husband and about six years as a single parent. After becoming accustomed to such independence, it was a challenge for Norma to suddenly be single with a two-year-old, struggling to make ends meet. She credits her father with being there when she needed him, whether to lend her money for an unexpected car repair or babysit her child in a pinch. Knowing a parent was there and ready to offer help if she needed it provided Norma a sense of security she would never forget. In many ways, Norma has adopted this approach as a parent. However a more hard-line model has also been beneficial at times.

When she turned thirty-five, Norma's stepmother encouraged her father to put an end to her three-year stipend. Norma was on her own. This decision was a good lesson, Norma says, because although she always paid her father back for money borrowed, his willingness to open his wallet did not teach her any hard lessons. "When he stopped helping me was when I really grew up."

My Observations

After dealing with her reservations about letting her son go, Norma laid out a clear plan to prepare her son for independent living. She correctly views the assistance she offered Seth in organizing his loan repayment schedule as necessary guidance, not enabling. Her son's belief that his mother was "nagging" him is natural and, in truth, beneficial. Without such friction many adult children are unable to leave the security of home.

Nate acted in the model of many biological fathers. His view of Seth as a capable adult balanced Norma's maternal instinct to protect him. Fortunately for their family, parental differences did not escalate to the point of injuring their marriage, which is not uncommon, especially when the adult child is in his thirties or forties.

Lessons Learned

The accounts of Melody and Norma reveal why it is necessary for some parents to rewrite the timetable for "emptying the nest." Both mothers knew that their adult children needed additional supports before taking on the mantle of independent living and that forcing them out prematurely would not work. Neither parent wanted nor expected her child to stay home forever. Rather they recognized the value of establishing clear expectations and coaching their children toward mature decision making.

As parents, it is important to find compromises with your children that they can live with. Finally, other adults in the same home, e.g., stepparents, can bring a fresh perspective; feedback that is contradictory to our own opinions often has merit and can lead to better understanding of our children and ourselves.

Here are some guidelines to help you through the process of your adult child's maturation:

1. There is no definitive age for moving out or getting one's career path established.

2. No matter how focused you are on your child's future, that future belongs to him or her. He or she may never have your vision of what life should be like.

3. Do your best to understand who your child is. That means conducting an honest appraisal of his or her strengths, challenges, and desires. Input from others is often helpful, as you cannot be totally objective.

4. There are times when it is appropriate and wise to insist that your adult child move out. Usually parents have gone through much strife by the time they reach that place.

5. Challenging times call upon parents to continue in their own growth. You may want to get the insights of professionals or other parents going through similar challenges.

6. Recognize that what you and your child are going through is a normal part of life, but that does not mean accepting behavior that is completely out of line (e.g., abusive, illegal).

7. Two good questions to ask yourself for clarity are: "Is what I am doing right now working?" and "How might I be contributing to the difficulties?"

8. There may be a multitude of reasons why one person is ready for independence sooner than another. Do not be too quick to judge yourself or your child.

CHAPTER TEN

- - - - - - - - - - - - - - -

"We Don't Talk Anymore"

Alienated Parents, Alienated Adult Children

There are many ways in which parents may become blindsided by unexpected calamities during the course of their lifetimes. For some, it is an obvious event that derails life as planned—death, illness, divorce, or a child's drug abuse. A more perplexing loss of innocence occurs when parents are alienated from their adult children with no apparent precipitating event. Instead of eagerly anticipating time with their children, these parents may shy away from intimacy, fearing disapproval or the rehashing of past events that cast them in a negative light. Those who lose contact with the child find themselves baffled, longing to repair what may be a permanently altered relationship. The impact of such estrangement varies from one parent to the next, but the common denominator is disillusionment, a tarnishing of their dreams of how life should be.

In this chapter, I've chosen to include the experiences of three mothers, who, voluntarily or not, have broken contact with their children. We will start with Samantha, whom I first interviewed in 2007.

Samantha

Samantha has been a single parent since her children were quite small. Her divorce was contentious, and animosity between her and her ex-husband remains to this day.

Her son and daughter, Alex and Allison, are twins. During their childhood and adolescence they spent the better part of each week with Samantha, visiting their father on alternate weekends and holidays. Both children excelled as student athletes and went on to receive college scholarships. Alex played baseball for the University of Texas, while Allison played basketball at San Diego State. It was a challenge for Samantha to keep up with their busy schedules, but she attended games as frequently as she could. Samantha works at home as a consultant for a major website developer. The job's flexibility has allowed her to stay highly involved in her children's lives.

To the outsider, Samantha's was a model family. Despite having grown up in two households, Alex and Allison thrived from a young age. Samantha is a natural problem-solver, who utilized this skill as a parent. She recognized problems in her parents' preferred discipline strategy—the silent treatment—and was determined to do things differently. She allowed her children to disagree with her, as long as they agreed to talk things through. When problems arose, her attitude was to identify the problem, then seek solutions through conversation and negotiation. Ignoring the issue was not an option.

Throughout most of the twins' school years, this approach worked. Samantha's focus was her children. She put dating on hold, success-fully campaigned for a seat on the school board, volunteered in her children's classes, and became a well-known figure in the community. She and her children remained close, until Alex and Allison entered high school and the family began the dance of differentiation.

Samantha had high expectations of her children. She insisted they strive to "be better than others," lest anyone claim they received special treatment because of her status in the community. Alex and Allison remained stellar students; however, they started pushing her limits in other ways. They wanted ever-later curfews, co-ed sleepovers, unlimited driving privileges. They wanted to be able to go out at night without checking in with her as to their whereabouts.

Samantha was scared. She feared for their safety and worried they might get out of control if given too much leeway. After a good deal of thought, she decided it best to set firm limits. However, that created a new problem: now she was worried her children would want to go live with their father, who was more lenient than she.

While Samantha knew she did not have complete control of her children, she wanted to be able to set reasonable restrictions on their social lives. In this regard, she was losing leverage. Her ex-husband enjoyed being the "good guy," allowing Alex and Allison more freedom, while casting Samantha as the villain. She tried to keep the conflict between her and her ex-husband to a minimum, but it was difficult. According to Samantha, he used every opportunity to speak critically of her and sabotage her relationship with her children. She was afraid if they lived with him, he would turn them against her, and with Allison that is exactly what happened.

By court order, both teenagers were required to live with their mother until high school graduation. Allison, however, began staying at her father's home in defiance. Samantha insisted that the court order be followed and that her daughter return home. Allison refused. Several weeks later Samantha awoke to noise on the street in front of her house. She initially thought it was the trash pickup, but soon realized curbside service wasn't scheduled until later in the week. When she looked out of her living room window she was startled to find a flatbed truck pulling away, and even more astounded to see twelve portable toilets in her driveway. Samantha called the company named on them and learned that an order had been placed for one dozen to be delivered to her address. Until she could straighten out the mess and have the toilets taken away, she was effectively blocked from leaving her home.

Her difficulties did not end there. Over the next three weeks numerous contractors arrived to give bids on new windows, siding, and gutters—none of which Samantha had scheduled. Never was there any admission as to who was responsible for the porta-potty incident, nor for the dispatching of multiple contractors to her home, but Samantha had her suspicions it was Allison.

Still, she was willing to forgive her daughter if that meant maintaining the relationship. Throughout the next week she left repeated phone messages and e-mails indicating that she loved her daughter and wanted to reconcile. She received no response. A few months later, when the twins left for college, Allison completely broke contact. Every few months Samantha sent gift packages and spending money to both children, but none of these gestures were acknowledged by her daughter. When I last spoke with Samantha, Allison and Alex had just graduated from their respective universities. Samantha attended both graduations, as did their father, but her daughter's reaction to seeing her was far from what she'd hoped.

On receiving her diploma, Allison thanked only her father, completely ignoring any contributions her mother had made to her successful completion of college. At dinner that evening, Allison barely spoke to her mother. Samantha was polite, but devastated by her daughter's coldness. She left as soon as she could.

Samantha's Observations

Samantha says Allison is like a former acquaintance to her now, someone she once knew, but no longer does. Doubtful about the prospect of reconciliation, she consoles herself with the knowledge she tried to take the "high road" and be consistent in showing love for her children. Her daughter has never apologized for her actions or attitude, nor has she taken any steps to reconcile.

To Samantha, her closeness to her children has been both a blessing and a curse. They loved her involvement with their school and extra-curricular activities until they reached adolescence, at which point they began to rebel. Allison, in particular, began to resent Samantha for not letting her live with her father. She accused her mother of being controlling and manipulative and, by her junior year in high school, displayed rudeness to her in public as well as at home. Samantha never expected that her daughter's rudeness would lead to total alienation, but it did. Now Samantha learns what Allison is doing only through her son.

With the benefit of hindsight, Samantha says, she would have interrupted the family's busy lifestyle when the twins were growing up, taking time to do more for others. She would have let Allison live with her father when she desired, rather than letting the custody battle go to court. Sadly, hindsight does not offer much solace in these situations.

Samantha's coping strategy during the last four years of estrangement from her daughter has been to attend counseling and stay involved with her family and a close circle of friends. To some degree, this has helped. Although she has experienced depression and anxiety as a result of the fractured relationship with her only daughter, she is moving forward with her life. She tries to put Allison out of her mind by keeping busy. Presently, there is no contact between the two.

My Observations

Samantha's experiences touch on several themes covered in this book. As a divorced woman with primary custody of her children, Samantha was in a position to become exceptionally close to her son and daughter. She not only worked from home but also was involved with the twins' scholastic and extracurricular activities. This closeness, which both children enjoyed when younger, frustrated them as they went through adolescence. Allison may have felt the need to push hard to differentiate from her mother. In addition, it appears that Allison's dad tacitly encouraged the divisiveness between her and her mother, in an effort to get closer to his daughter. It is possible that Allison's father intentionally or inadvertently conveyed the message to her that she could not have a relationship with both parents. She obviously chose to place her affections with her father.

In trying to show unconditional love for both twins, Samantha's relationship with her daughter became severely out of balance. By continuing to send her gifts, money, positive notes, and voice messages with no expectation of civil treatment in return, Samantha allowed herself to be taken for granted and disrespected. Allison rebuffed her repeatedly, was hostile to her in their few contacts, yet there were never any consequences for her actions, such as a moratorium on gift-giving. Samantha could still love her daughter and let her experience the natural consequences that her behavior warranted. Unconditional love does not mean tolerating abuse. *It is completely appropriate to pull back when treated poorly.*

Samantha has had to grieve several losses, including the affections of the mother-daughter relationship and her dream of being in her daughter's future. Although she still has contact with Alex, there is awkwardness whenever Allison's name comes up, as Alex deliberately avoids talking about his sister and their father. Fortunately, Samantha has good coping skills. In addition to getting more actively involved in her career, she has taken up tennis and started dating. Having survived multiple anxiety attacks and radio silence from her daughter, Samantha believes she has progressed through the darkest period and is ready to move on. At this point she is done trying to make amends.

But, like other parents, she had to "stay the course" with her attempts at reconciliation, as long as she felt she could. No one else could make that decision for her.

Vanessa

Vanessa is in her early sixties. A positive person by nature, she had expectations as a young wife that she would be a stay-at-home mother to her three children. For years her image of herself was that of "volunteer queen and chauffeur" to her children and their school. However, when her husband's job proved less stable than anticipated she returned to work. At the time, her youngest child was just going into kindergarten. Vanessa was angry. She resisted the idea of returning to work, but the family's living expenses required her to return to her former job as a court reporter.

Now, years later, she acknowledges that returning to work was a good thing. She made lifelong friendships, improved her professional skills, and assumed a pivotal role in the community. Her husband coached their son's sports teams and stayed active in their daughters' varied interests: Girl Scouts, gymnastics, and dance. Once all three children had gone on to college, Vanessa felt comfortable claiming she and Tom had done a good job as parents and earned the right to be empty nesters.

The lives of their children have diverged upon entering the adult years. Vanessa's oldest daughter is career oriented and made it clear, early on, she did not want to have a family. After college she enlisted in the military, a decision Vanessa is happy with as it has afforded her daughter the opportunity to travel and experience life abroad. Things have not gone as smoothly in the lives of her other children, largely due to jealousy. Robert, two years Evelyn's junior, excelled at everything he did, and while Vanessa and her husband strived to affirm the strengths of each of their children, Evelyn grew to resent her brother's successes. Vanessa hoped this would pass as they matured into adults. It didn't.

When Robert announced rather suddenly that he was going to get married, the entire family was surprised. They were even more surprised when Evelyn made her own wedding announcement amid the preparations. To Vanessa's dismay, the wedding date Evelyn and her fiancé, Gary, chose predated Robert's, a decision Vanessa believes Evelyn made as a way of upstaging her brother.

The dueling marriage dates led to friction between Robert and Evelyn, but Vanessa and her husband were happy for both children and wisely stayed out of the fray. Within a couple years both their younger two children became parents. New wrinkles began to surface. Evelyn and her husband were very protective of their young son. At one point, Vanessa says, she was chastised for giving her grandson a sip of pop during a lengthy car ride. It wasn't so much her daughter's correcting her, but the severity of the correction that bothered Vanessa: "If you cannot do what I want, you can get out of the car!" Similar reprimands were made at other times with equal vehemence. Evelyn and Gary gradually pulled away from Vanessa, seldom inviting her and her husband to their new home.

Vanessa hoped that a Christmas visit would bridge the gap. To her dismay, the visit began and ended with a brisk encounter with her son-in-law. Upon entering the house, she was immediately told to wash her hands. She disregarded the comment. She and her husband were well, as was her grandson. There was no need to worry about passing germs to the toddler. When she and Tom left, her son-in-law asked if she had heard him when he'd told her to wash her hands.

"Yes, I did," Vanessa said.

"And you chose to ignore me?" he asked sharply.

Other similarly tense encounters increased the divide between Vanessa and daughter. After missing their grandson's birthday while out of town, Vanessa and her husband returned home to an angry phone call: "What kind of grandparents are you?" Evelyn asked with contempt.

There was no making up for this affront. Vanessa and Tom's repeated invitations to Evelyn and her family were declined. The two parents were ignored on their birthdays. Mother's and Father's Day passed without a word. The following year, still unsure what she had done wrong, Vanessa decided to try something new. She would let her daughter be ignored on *her* birthday. Evelyn's birthday went unacknowledged and, not surprisingly, when Vanessa's next birthday came around, a gift from Evelyn appeared at her doorstep.

Vanessa has repeatedly apologized to her daughter and still does not understand what fatal flaw she has committed. When she tries talking to Evelyn, she is met with comments like, "Oh, so now you want to tell me how to live my life." Eventually, Vanessa sought counseling. The therapist asked her if she wanted to "be close to Evelyn, or to be right." Preferring, of course, to be close, Vanessa again took responsibility for initiating attempts at reconciliation. But the relationship has never returned to what it was.

Vanessa's Observations

Vanessa has given the situation much thought. She is tired of blaming herself, drained from her repeated efforts to win over her daughter's good graces. She wonders if her son-in-law, whom she initially thought of as a gentle, lighthearted soul, has encouraged Evelyn to shun her. Her hope is that the long Cold War is only a phase, but she realizes this is unlikely.

Reflecting on her history with Evelyn, Vanessa remembers a time before the wedding during which she and her daughter attended beading workshops and jewelry shows together. Evelyn advised her mother on choices of paints, wallpaper, and home accessories, and Vanessa cherished her daughter's suggestions. Although she holds out hope that one day she and her daughter can be close again, she is doubtful that will happen. Vanessa says she continues to grieve the loss of the relationship that she once had with Evelyn, but her days of apologizing are done. "I decided I can't do this anymore. Now I want to be right."

My Observations

Their estrangement from Evelyn is something of a mystery to Vanessa and Tom. They've searched themselves and their family's history to uncover how and where the unraveling began. Evelyn's jealousy of her brother seems to figure into the equation, as well as her difficulty making the transition into an adult relationship with her parents. As noted earlier, some adult children who are very close to a parent do not emancipate easily, at least not emotionally. Their dependence on an emotional level is seen in behavior that looks just like its opposite: independence and hostility. *If one has to constantly remind others that she runs her own life, then she likely has doubts about her actual ability to do so.*

When parents reflect on such children, they often remember a child growing up who kept a running tabulation of what he received from his parents, versus what a sibling had obtained. If this child feels that he has been slighted by a parent, he may hold a grudge indefinitely. Parents who indulge their children's complaints about them (e.g., the perceived wrongdoings) fall into a trap that perpetuates an unhealthy interaction. The parent assumes a position of guilt, and when she tries to get back into her child's good graces through apologies and overtures, the child misunderstands the apology as an admission of wrongdoing. Such a parent has few, if any, expectations of her child, to whom she cedes control of the relationship. The parent is left like a beggar holding out her cup in the hope of charity.

In Vanessa's case, she grew tired of this unhealthy cycle and decided to interrupt it. She did not have to be rude or hostile herself to achieve this, but she did have to let her daughter know that she had some basic expectations for how she wishes to be treated.

Deanna

Deanna is divorced. She has a twenty-eight-year-old son named Troy. She and her husband, Greg, split when Troy was seven years old, and for many years she raised him as a single parent. She became pregnant with Troy just five months into the marriage. By that time she recognized that her husband was "cruel and sadistic," but she was determined to have her child and forge a positive family life.

That did not happen. Her husband's disrespect for her ultimately led to the nullification of their marriage. He challenged her for custody of Troy, even though she was the one who took primary care of him throughout his childhood. During the custody dispute, Troy came home with distressing stories of how he defended her reputation to his father when he called her a "bitch." And there were other sources of conflict. Deanna claims she paid for more than her share of expenses, including all of Troy's clothes. Worse still, when she sent clothes to her ex-husband's home with him, the clothing never came back.

Eventually, the custody battle worked out in Deanna's favor. Troy spent most of his time with her and by the time he was a teenager, the two were very close. Deanna was happy with the way her life was shaping up. She was able to advance in her career as a university

administrator, while continuing to meet the needs of her son. However, when Troy turned fifteen, the nature of their relationship
began to change. Deanna took Troy on a ten-day trip to Peru, to see
Machu Picchu and fulfill what was for her a life's dream. She thought
Troy was old enough and had tastes similar enough to her own to
appreciate such a vacation. She was wrong. Troy liked almost nothing
about the trip. "He was awful and depressed. I felt like the ultimate
cheerleader," she told me in frustration. He complained for years
afterward about the hot weather, the "boring" historic sites, and their
not spending enough time in the big cities. Deanna was crestfallen:
this was the beginning of her son's withdrawal.

Shortly after their return, Deanna met another man, Ray, whom
she ultimately married. Ray and Troy had a good relationship. He had
children of his own, so Troy had siblings for the first time. Ray often
mediated the conflicts between Deanna and her son. "Troy was a good
kid. He never did drugs," Deanna says. "But like many teenagers he
knew how to push my buttons."

Deanna and Ray's marriage came to an abrupt end when Ray revealed just a few years into the marriage that he wanted a divorce.
The news came as a shock to both Deanna and Troy. When Troy called
his stepfather, asking him to stay in his life, the call was ignored. He
never heard from Ray again. Deanna suffered not only for herself but
for her son as well. Cut off from the most significant male role model
in his life, Troy's irritability with his mother intensified.

Recently, Troy married a young woman, and since the wedding he
has grown increasingly cool toward his mother. Deanna feels she has
been thrown into an unspoken competition with her new in-laws, in
which she is compared unfavorably against Troy's mother-in-law and
blamed for any problems the young couple has. She has sought counseling, and invited her son to attend therapy with her. So far he has
not taken her up on the offer. In fact, the friction between Deanna
and Troy has escalated nearly to the point at which the two no longer
have any contact. In the rare times Troy does speak to his mother, it
is only when he needs something. Recently, she lent him money for
a deposit on his first home: "This is a kid I fought to have, I fought to
keep, and provided as solid and nurturing an upbringing as possible.
When I had him, for the first time in my life, I thought, 'Now I have
a family; now I have love.' So when he was such a jerk it was a loss."

Deanna had major surgery a year ago. Throughout her entire stay in the hospital, her son and his wife did not once call to see how she was doing. Rather than remain alone after her surgery, she called upon close friends to come visit her. Many stayed for days at a time. Upon release she needed a ride home, and Troy and his wife frigidly told her to get a cab, as they had plans for the day. Their withdrawal from her life bordered on abandonment. Several months later Deanna's home was damaged following a severe snowstorm. She called her son for help. Once again, his schedule was so tied up she had to rely on others for help.

This entire experience has saddened and angered Deanna, but she does not give up easily. Recently, she turned fifty-five. Predictably, Troy said nothing about her birthday. She went ahead and celebrated with her close friends. Days later, when she still had not heard from him, she left several messages on his voice mail. Her calls went unreturned. She left a final message: "Troy, it breaks my heart when you don't answer your phone." He returned this call. She told him how hurt she was that he had not even sent her a card.

Within a couple days Deanna was invited to the couple's home for a birthday dinner, with flowers and a cake. Though she felt mildly insulted the event did not happen without her prompting, she considered the evening a success. She felt more connected to her son than she had in a long time, and was comfortable interacting with his wife. After dinner, when a travel documentary about Machu Picchu happened to air on TV, she and Troy recollected their South America trip. With added years of life experience and maturity, Troy was able to appreciate his mother's thoughtfulness in taking him to the historic site. "At last," Deanna said, "I have reason to be hopeful."

Deanna's Observations

Reflecting on how her relationship with her son has evolved, Deanna says she is in a more positive place now, glad she never gave him ultimatums or used guilt as leverage to win his companionship. There were many times she thought of lashing out at her son verbally but refrained from doing so: "Don't under any circumstances deliberately do anything yourself that closes the door on a relationship, even though it is incredibly tempting." She believes she and Troy were probably on the verge, at times, of severing ties completely, but stresses that relationships go through stages of relative closeness and separation: "Circumstances do change; kids mature; we change. The things that once were mountains still hurt, but I've got a life of my own, so he doesn't have as much power over me now."

My Observations

Given that the majority of Troy's childhood was spent exclusively with Deanna in a single-parent household, their relationship was especially close. Without her encouraging him to do so, Troy became the protector of his mother. His biological father tried to diminish her standing in Troy's eyes with insults and name-calling. Initially, this strategy backfired. As a pre-adolescent, Troy defended Deanna against his father's verbal assaults. Since Troy was closer to Deanna than to anyone else in his world, it was natural that he would side with her.

However, a few years later, during the "dance of differentiation," Troy developed an antagonistic attitude toward his mother. For children who grow up in single-parent households, such dissension can be especially acute since there is generally only one parent from whom to emancipate and that parent bears the brunt of the child's animosity and frustration. Troy is now in his late twenties. His recent softening attitude toward his mother likely indicates he is moving successfully through the separation and individuation process. He no longer has to prove his independence to her or to himself.

Another factor influencing Troy's behavior toward his mother is his lack of appropriate male role models. Deanna's older brother lives across the country and does not see his nephew often. At one point Deanna called him in desperation, seeking advice about her son's unwillingness to help her with some unfinished home projects. He called Troy and admonished him for being unappreciative and inappropriate. Shortly thereafter, Troy offered his assistance. The lesson: when another male role model finally called Troy on his behavior, it changed very quickly.

Lessons Learned

All three mothers in this chapter felt close to their children in early childhood, which is part of the reason why the change in their children's attitudes was so distressing. In best-case scenarios, the discord between a parent and child resolves itself in the late teenage years or early adulthood. But as we are seeing throughout this book, that is not always the case. Particularly for baby boomer parents, the separation and individuation process can be slow and painful. The reasons for this are not easily summarized, but it is safe to say there is rarely one calamitous event that turns a child against her parent.

In these examples, none of the mothers made the mistake of using guilt to compel their children to be closer to them; however, they did err by allowing themselves to be used. It is often difficult for mothers to gauge healthy boundaries between themselves and their children, which is one of the reasons talking to others and getting input from a third party can be beneficial.

When parents become alienated from their children, a mixture of personal preference and outside opinion should dictate how to proceed. The best outcomes occur when the young adult no longer needs to push so defiantly against a parent. This may happen through maturation, the passage of time, or an event such as a serious illness or death that brings the family closer together. Even when reconcilement does not occur, parents can and do go on.

Here are some suggestions for handling alienation, if that is what you are experiencing:

1. Listen to your adult child's point of view, but do not automatically assume his or her stance. Nor should you automatically assume you have no responsibility for the problem.

2. Request more information: "It seems like you are so disappointed in me all the time. Help me understand what this is about."

3. Even if you disagree with your adult child's thoughts and feelings, remember that they are valid in your son or daughter's mind. Acknowledging their validity does not mean you have to agree with them.

4. Indicate a willingness to listen, but clarify your expectations: "I'd like to hear your point of view, but I need to feel safe during our conversation. Please talk civilly."

5. If his or her behavior is too upsetting (due to yelling, swearing, or threatening language, for example) end the conversation: "This kind of contact doesn't work for me. Call me when you can speak in a more normal tone."

6. Do not be too readily available. If you are constantly the "giver" in the relationship, your child may come to question your worth.

7. Be honest about your feelings, but avoid using guilt as a tool for leverage. It usually doesn't work.

8. Avoid "you" messages. Instead of "you make me feel bad when you're so critical of me," try, "I like getting together and want to do so, but I end up feeling distant when you constantly tell me what I am doing wrong."

9. Offer to go to counseling with your adult child to get the viewpoint of a third party. Be willing to take responsibility for your half of the relationship and work on your own issues. If your son or daughter will not go, find a therapist and go on your own.

10. If the relationship seems beyond repair, even with your very best efforts, grieve the loss and move forward. Get support and find other people and activities that will fill the vacancy left in your child's absence.

- - - - - - - - - - - - - - - - -

CHAPTER ELEVEN

"What to Do as a Stepparent"

Blended Family Matters

Parenting a spouse's or partner's children is becoming increasingly common. Millions of households now experience so-called blended families—in fact, the US Census Bureau,[1] in 2004, reported that seventeen percent of all children (12.2 million) under the age of eighteen lived in such families. Characterized by remarriage or by children in a household who share one or no biological parents, blended families confront the ordinary challenges of the nuclear family along with additional concerns worth examining here:

1. You are not going to have the same connection to your stepchildren as you do with your own kids. As much as you love your stepchildren, the bond is different from the one you have with your child. That goes for your partner or spouse as well.

1. Each individual coming into a blended family has his or her needs and agenda. While stepparents may hope to establish close bonds, their stepchildren may have different ideas about the level of intimacy they desire. Adolescents, especially, are in a stage of emotional withdrawal from their parents and frequently crave space to forge their own identities.

2. Parents may have special challenges responding to the new family structure. Their affection toward each other will not necessarily be mirrored in the relationships between stepsiblings or between a child and his or her stepparent. Children of all ages may see the new parent, not as a welcome addition to the family, but as someone who

interrupts the existing family dynamic; and a child may not want to share his biological parent with either the new parent or the stepsiblings.

3. Families from dissimilar value systems, life experiences, and standards of living often clash when working through their differences. A teen-ager who has had to work for perks like tickets to concerts, designer clothes, and cars will likely be troubled by a stepbrother accustomed to getting whatever he asks for with no expectations from his parents. These differences carry over into adulthood and shape relationships among family members. Even if it is not openly discussed, an undercurrent of jealousy, perceived unfairness, and scorekeeping may pervade in these relationships.

4. Stepparents can be more objective than biological parents in assessing the potential outcomes of a parenting decision. Biological parents often have a more difficult time saying "no" to their children, and hearing a different perspective can keep the parent from overindulging, particularly when it comes to money lending. If the relationship between the biological parent and his or her child becomes strained, a stepparent can serve as a bridge between the parent and child, or, alternatively, help the parent with the task of letting go.

5. A nonbiological parent may see an adult stepchild as mature and capable when the biological parent cannot. What may start as a conflict between the couple can then become a positive: a stepfather may encourage his spouse to look at her daughter through his eyes and realize she deserves to be treated as an adult, not a child.

6. A stepparent chooses to make a new family unit with his or her spouse; the couple's children, including their adult children, make no such choice. If a lasting connection blossoms from the union, it should be celebrated as a blessing. If it does not, a parent should make his or her best effort at treating the spouse's children respectfully, recognizing limits in what he or she can expect from the relationship.

7. Many stepparents and their stepchildren form strong bonds as friends. Be open to that possibility. When it occurs it is very rewarding. As a parent or stepparent, you are always positioned to be a positive influence in another's life and reap the benefits of a new friendship.

The stories below illustrate two distinct ways of coping with the blended family issue.

Cathy

Cathy came into Steve's life when the two were middle aged. Cathy, who never had children of her own, now finds herself with four grown children and two grandchildren. She's bonded easily with the children, and feels so connected to their lives she never refers to them as her stepchildren—they are simply her children.

Steve and his first wife, Diane, divorced twenty years before Cathy met him. For many years his kids lived primarily with their mother, and Steve saw them only on weekends and holidays. Cathy believes they have had a cloistered life under the instruction of their mother, whose philosophy, she says, is "Life is good. God will provide. I will protect you." In Cathy's mind, it has been she and Steve who have done the providing.

Over the years Cathy and Steve have helped the children through financially tough times. Though they've always been glad to be supportive, giving away money is becoming more difficult now as they approach their retirement years. The kids seem to view them as the "Bank of Mom and Dad," while, from Cathy's standpoint, the children's mother and stepfather are assuming the role of "warm and fuzzy" parents. Cathy says, "I can't buy new furniture or take a vacation because we have given so much to the kids." The decision as to where to draw the line is beginning to strain her relationship with her husband.

Her stepchildren are now in their twenties and thirties, and all but one—Elliot—appear to be successfully launched. Cathy calls him their "nine-month kid" because every nine months there is a new crisis in Elliot's life. Elliot's struggle began in his first year of college. To make up for his sheltered high school years, he partied relentlessly for nine months, failed all his classes, and did not return to school.

Since then, Elliot has gone from job to job, transitioning in and out of Steve and Cathy's home multiple times. Elliot lived with Cathy for several months while Steve was working in Hong Kong. He appeared to be leading a more stable life, until Cathy made a trip to visit Steve over the winter holidays. Four days before Christmas they received a call at 4:00 a.m. Hong Kong time: Elliot was locked out of the house with no coat and no money. Cathy called a friend who had a key to the house. She drove through snow piled a foot deep to let Elliot in and make sure he had food.

When Steve returned home from the Far East, Elliot's life improved. He got a new job and his own apartment. He found a new girlfriend, Laci. Cathy and Steve would not give him money or co-sign on a loan for a car, but they helped coach him through negotiations with a car dealer. Elliot seemed to be managing well and acquiring some independence.

Then a new crisis erupted. Elliot called one day in a panic. He had come home from work to find the police at his apartment. They were arresting Laci for alleged credit card theft and computer fraud. Elliot knew she had been using his computer at night, but was given the impression she was chatting with friends online. He could not believe she lied to him. To his surprise, Laci admitted hacking into strangers' accounts. Worse, she claimed that he was in on it. After all, he had let her use his computer. Elliot's computer was seized, and Elliot and Laci were arrested. Cathy and Steve hurried to the St. Louis jail where Elliot was being held, and secured his bail. Elliot would need a criminal defense lawyer to contest the charges. Retaining one would cost several thousand dollars, an amount which put a significant dent in Cathy and Steve's retirement savings. When word reached Elliot's employer about his legal problems, he was promptly laid off.

Cathy views payment of the attorney's retainer as a moral necessity: a loan, not a gift, for her troubled son. Steve evidently thinks otherwise. Elliot has verbally agreed to pay them at least $50 per month, but has made no effort to formalize the agreement in writing. Historically, Cathy has worked to limit monetary gifts to the children, but having grandchildren has made it harder to say "no." Nevertheless, what has happened with Elliot has motivated her to set firmer boundaries. When asked to pay for his college classes (Elliot plans to return to school), Cathy told her son she would reimburse him after he successfully completed his coursework.

Cathy has tried to be supportive, but her patience is waning, particularly for Elliot's attitude. He speaks to her nonchalantly, as if his legal problems have vanished: "It's all behind me now. Nothing bad is going to happen to me." Cathy and Steve think differently. They worry not only about him, but about their financial future. Their son "is immature, always has excuses for his situations, and doesn't take accountability." Cathy wants to see that change.

Cathy's Observations

Cathy and Steve are the sandwiched generation, compelled to help not only their developing children but also their deteriorating parents. All four of their parents, still living, are increasingly needy. Cathy knows that eventually they will have at least one set of parents living with them. She hopes her children are launched into responsible adult lives before then, however that is far from certain.

To cope with managing a job and various family pressures, Cathy relies on the support of her faith and friends. She has learned to accept undesirable circumstances, as well as ask for help when she needs it. Her friends help keep her on track by giving advice she might not be able to accept from others.

It has not been easy to launch four children, but, for the most part, Cathy has maintained a good relationship with them. "How many step-moms," she jokes, "are asked by all four of their kids to be their friends on Facebook?"

My Observations

From the time I met her two years ago, Cathy has always spoken well of her stepchildren. What stood out to me from early on was her ability to avoid "knee-jerk" acquiescence to her adult children's financial wishes. She offered balance to her husband's perspective, whose lifelong attachment to Elliot made it more difficult for him to resist immediately granting his requests. Unforeseen crises in the children's lives led them to put more pressure on Cathy and Steve for help, who have provided it within reasonable limits.

Elliot, the "nine-month" child, presents a pattern of unstable decision-making. Continuing to financially rescue him is wrong for two reasons: first, Elliot will not bear the weight of the consequences for his actions.

He still seems to have difficulty connecting the dots—saying, for instance, his legal problems are "all behind me." He owes his parents a debt for the money they loaned him for the attorney's retainer; that is not behind him. Second, the money is running out. Elliot has needed more support than his siblings. If he is tried in court, do his parents have the responsibility to continue paying legal fees at the expense of their ability to retire? No. Even if they did decide to keep the money flowing in his direction, it is likely Elliot's siblings would take issue with the inequitable distribution of their parents' funds.

The most difficult challenge for Cathy and Steve may be to accept that Elliot may never have the kind of life they had hoped for him. Hard-working parents long to see their adult children thrive. The truth is that some do not. Only Cathy and Steve can know how much and what kind of help to give and when to do so.

Rebecca

Rebecca was a single mother when she married Randy, an engineer. They each had two teenage daughters. The children are now grown and moved out, and the daughters are married. Rebecca is the daughter of German immigrants and the granddaughter of Holocaust victims. She grew up in a home governed by an Old World style of parenting, where children were to listen, not to be heard. It was an unspoken household rule that no one should ever bring up or discuss Germany, and no one did.

Tragedy struck when Rebecca was fourteen and her father died in a car accident. Her mother had never talked about her feelings—neither about her husband's early death nor the death of her own parents. While Rebecca herself does not practice such a constrained parenting style, she admires her mother's strength.

In raising her own family, Rebecca is a self-described "processor" of events and emotions. She has read books such as *Children: the Challenge*,[2] by Rudolph Dreikurs and Vicki Soltz, to guide her parenting decisions. She gives her children choices, encourages them to think through their actions, and follows up with appropriate consequences. While her own parents were direct and authoritarian,

Rebecca is tolerant and open to negotiation. Driven by a desire to build consensus, she sees herself as a flexible parent who is willing to compromise with her children.

When Rebecca and Randy married they experienced what they thought were the normal stresses of blending two families. It later became clear there were some unresolved issues at stake with regard to Randy's divorce and remarriage. After sixteen years of marriage to Rebecca, Randy had a disagreement with his daughters over the circumstances of his divorce. The dispute snowballed and divided the family. Soon after, the daughters announced they needed a sabbatical from both their father and stepmother. Randy and Rebecca were shocked. They asked for family counseling, and Randy's daughters agreed to meet a therapist with their father. The results were unsuccessful. Tension spilled over into Rebecca's and Randy's marriage—not only did they lose contact with the girls, but contact with their grandson was severed as well. Randy, especially, was hurting.

But, as sometimes happens, crisis opened a locked door. About two years later, Randy's daughter, Yvette, became pregnant and gave birth to a little girl. To assist in what was to be a difficult pregnancy and labor, Yvette welcomed her father back into her life. Rebecca, however, was not welcome, and Randy was asked to spend time at both of his daughters' homes without his wife.

Another crisis occurred, about one year later, when Randy's elderly mother suddenly died. Without a word of discussion Rebecca was accepted back into the good graces of the family. The ease of their forgiveness was a mystery to her, as she was accustomed to talking things through slowly. She had envisioned the need for a serious conversation to soften the feelings of ill-will between herself and her stepdaughters, but that never took place. A door had been opened, and she needed to step through it. The three-year sabbatical was put to an end.

Still, the estrangement had taken a toll on Rebecca and Randy, as well as their stepchildren. The two sets of stepsiblings have not reestablished any relationship, and Rebecca and Randy continue to celebrate holidays with each set of children separately. It is not an ideal arrangement, but for now it is the best Rebecca can hope for. She has come to terms with the boundaries the family has drawn, and she'll be content even if the situation never changes.

Rebecca's Observations

Recently, I asked Rebecca how she coped during the three years of estrangement. She said she was very angry at times; at other times, just quite hurt. When Randy was let back in, she was relieved for him, but another year of being excluded from this side of the family took its toll on her. "I couldn't stand that feeling in the pit of my stomach." She decided that she was not going to stay dragged down forever. So she began to work on letting go. Rebecca went to counseling with her husband, and alone. She maintained her close friendships and became involved in a diabetes fundraising organization. Her volunteer experiences gave her the perspective she needed.

Rebecca realized she had the perfect model for accepting things and letting go: her mother. Through the loss of her parents in the Holocaust and the death of her first and second husbands, her mother had become accustomed to grieving, accepting, and detaching from her losses. Eventually, Rebecca was able to cut free of her own anger and hurt. But it hasn't been easy. She has had to summon strength from her friends, her volunteer work, and the very core of her being. A psychologist told her years ago, "If you can live by these three statements, you will have a healthy, happy life: 'Accept yourself, control only yourself, and expect only of yourself.'" These guideposts have helped her through the sabbatical.

My Observations

Throughout the three years of her estrangement from her stepdaughters, Rebecca appeared to take the high road. She found ways to address her feelings through a team of her friends, sister, mother-in-law, therapist, and physician. Rebecca had a solid sense of self before the conflict began, which helped her learn to cope. She came to realize that her influence on the situation was quite limited— she could not make use of her interpersonal skills if her stepdaughters wanted nothing to do with her. But she could and did use her skills toward rewarding volunteer work. Over time this led her to the realization that she could have a full and meaningful life even if reconciliation did not occur.

Although shaken by the three-year sabbatical, Rebecca's positive self-image and outlook have allowed her to find lessons in the experience. She has strengthened her sense of self and reaffirmed her commitment to her values. She did not wait for reconciliation to get on with her life. She made a decision and moved on.

Lessons Learned

One of the strengths that both women displayed in getting through their respective situations was having strong support systems. They did not rely solely on their spouses for solace, which would have been problematic, as both husbands were even more closely attached to the children in crisis and could not possibly be objective. Both women chose to focus their energies internally and work on themselves with the help of friends or counselors.

They have wisely adjusted their expectations to the reality of their families. Cathy realizes that Elliot has a long way to go toward emotional maturity. In the meantime, she has made provisions for her own financial future. Rebecca understands the difference between her desire for closure and the ability of her stepdaughters to offer it. She also has come to accept that the entire blended family–two parents, four adult children and their families—might never have the unity she'd once hoped for.

Finally, we see that each of the two women featured in this chapter has restricted influence. As just one of the many ingredients in the composition of the family, a parent must realize her limited power to singlehandedly effect change.

If you are a stepparent struggling to find your place in the stepfamily dynamic, here are a few reminders to help you provide the most effective support to your stepchild:

1. Expect the unexpected in your family's relationships, whether biological or blended.

2. There are no recipes for guaranteed success. Sometimes we have to

redefine what "success" means: It could be the complete healing a severed relationship or simply healing oneself and moving forward.

3. A strong support system helps in any crisis situation.

4. Wanting something for your adult stepchild does not mean he or she will want it as well.

5. Staying respectful of your partner and his or her children is a key to getting through difficult times. You will have fewer regrets or relationships to mend if you are assertive and respectful.

6. Growing pains are normal for both biological and blended families. Try to look for and take note of healthy patterns that are present. You can be realistic and expect positive outcomes at the same time.

CHAPTER TWELVE

"I Wasn't Prepared For This"

Gender Orientation

We never really know what life has in store for us. Fortunate parents are those who meet what is unexpected with enthusiasm and an open heart and come to terms with it. For some parents, this means accepting a child's gender orientation and preference.

Gay and lesbian relationships have reached an unprecedented level of acceptance in America, but sadly prejudices still exist and a certain amount of stigma still surrounds some who openly claim an alternative sexual identity. One of the challenges for parents of LGBT (lesbian, gay, bisexual and transgendered) people is the fear that their child's sexual orientation will engender unfair treatment, or worse, result in physical or emotional injury. Furthermore, parents worry that they, too, may be rejected or treated differently by friends, family, or coworkers.

All of the major professional mental health organizations in America have affirmed that homosexuality is not a mental disorder. The American Psychiatric Association (APA)[1] removed homosexuality from its official diagnostic manual in 1973, and in 1998 the organization issued a statement to leaders and advocacy groups in other countries, urging them to abandon laws that penalize the private behavior of gay, lesbian, and bisexual adults. Recent publications from the APA indicate that sexual orientation develops across a lifetime. A young person may develop a sense of being heterosexual, gay, lesbian, or bisexual in childhood or adolescence, yet wait to reveal this knowledge for years or even decades, either because of uncertainty about his or her feelings, or out of fear of the social consequences of disclosure. When revelation of an alternative sexual orientation is made in early adulthood, parents may be caught off guard, especially if they have come to understand their child as heterosexual.

The journey toward accepting one's sexual orientation can be lengthy. There are those who have difficulty with this process for personal or religious reasons. Some enter into what is called reparative or conversion therapy. These therapies touch at the heart of the question as to whether sexual orientation can be changed. Faith-based change therapies employ a combination of journaling, biblical readings, individual counseling, and group discussion with the aim of discouraging homosexual behavior and attraction. Early conversion therapies also utilized what is known as "aversive conditioning" to extinguish homosexual attraction and induce heterosexual feelings. For example, they paired the presentation of homoerotic stimuli with nausea-inducing drugs, in an effort to eradicate the participants' homosexual feelings. The APA[2] denies the effectiveness of such therapies (which have been mostly discontinued), and many psychologists go further and say that the aversive therapies are in fact harmful. The APA does recognize, however, the effectiveness of "Gay Affirmative Psychotherapy," a type of therapy focused on overcoming stigmatization.

Families of LGBT can give and receive support through organizations such as PFLAG—Parents, Families and Friends of Lesbians and Gays. With around five hundred chapters across the country, PFLAG is a national, non-profit alliance guided by tolerance for diverse sexual orientations and gender identities. One of its aims is to provide support and advocacy for parents of LGBT children. PFLAG stresses that the range of emotions these parents experience is normal: they may feel confused, sad, and frightened; hurt their child is not the person they hoped him or her to be; worried about his or her future and well-being. PFLAG lets parents know they are not alone in their journey to better understand their children's sexual orientation and respond to it with sensitivity.

In the stories of Arianna and Leslie, we find two very different reactions from women who each learned of their child's alternative sexual orientation.

Arianna

Sixty-three-year-old Arianna has had surprises both at the beginning of her son's life and at the beginning of his adulthood. As a young woman, Arianna trained to be a nurse and moved from the Midwest to the West Coast to pursue her career. Like many women in the late 1960s, she frequented bohemian night spots friendly to the counterculture, including Sergeant Pepper's Lonely Hearts Club in San Francisco. There, she met her first husband, Trenton, who was soon to leave the navy. They married after a year of dating, and in two years Arianna gave birth to Derrick. Arianna was excited to embrace parenthood, but apparently Trenton was not. When Derrick was just three months old, his father left them. That first year as a young single mother was hard on Arianna, whose parents lived halfway across the country and could not offer much support. Arianna made it clear to Trenton that she expected him to be consistently involved in Derrick's life or she would fight for sole custody. His father agreed. Arianna stayed single for five years until she met and married, Ben, her current husband.

As Derrick grew up, Arianna noticed he was into what she called "non-boy stuff." Unlike other boys his age he showed no interest in sports, no interest in firemen or policemen. That alone was not terribly unusual, but there were other factors that distinguished Derrick:.he was more social than his male peers, and he preferred the company of girls to boys. Arianna, unconcerned about his gender orientation, thought he was just a late bloomer. But after high school Derrick moved east to attend Penn State. And it was there, just before returning home to California for Christmas break, that he called Arianna and informed her he was gay.

In that one conversation, her dream of Derrick living with a wife and grandkids was dashed. She says, "It was kind of a shock. My first thought was that he would die of AIDS." She cried and prayed that just the right woman would change him. After an hour or so, she realized that her tears were futile and selfish. Derrick was in the midst of a huge internal shift and her self-pity would not help. His greatest fear, she learned shortly thereafter, was not that he would be rejected, but that he would hurt her. He knew that in being authentic, he had shattered her expectations for his life.

While Derrick worried about his mother, she became increasingly concerned he would lead a lonely and depressed life. That was not the case at all. Derrick found open acceptance in the gay community at his school. Arianna was the one who, at least initially, had trouble adjusting.

Eventually, she decided to tell Derrick's father their son was gay. She did so without her son's knowledge, and Trenton did not take the news well. When father and son saw each other at Christmas, the first thing he uttered to Derrick was: "I heard some disturbing news from your mother." Their conversation deteriorated into a screaming match, and the relationship was cantankerous for years. Then one day Derrick received a call from his father, who was driving from Los Angeles to San Francisco, where Derrick now lived. He wanted to meet his son for a drink. The meeting turned out to be a blessing. The two talked openly about Derrick's sexuality and eventually found peace with each other. Perhaps Derrick's father knew his health was uncertain and wanted to make amends in the short time he had left. Only a few weeks later he died of undiagnosed pneumonia.

Derrick, for his part, is an active advocate for gay rights. He communicates routinely with legislators in Congress on the issue of gay marriage, and has interviewed candidates for political office on gay issues. On weekends he is an urban farmer with his partner. The two supply organic produce to restaurants in the Bay Area, and plan to open their own restaurant someday. During the week Derrick is an architectural engineer. His sexual orientation is not at the foreground of his life. Arianna does not want her son to be judged on this one aspect of his life, and so she chooses to share information about his sexuality only among people with whom she is close.

As parents often do with gender-identity issues, Arianna has looked inward at her parenting, wondering if some of her actions led to Derrick's unconventional orientation. She has come to the conclusion, to the contrary, that, "It's just the way the genes arranged themselves." She once asked Derrick if he regrets being gay, to which he, in a similar fashion of acceptance, replied, "No, Mom, it's just the way I am."

Arianna's Observations

Arianna was not brought up in a religion that condemned homosexuality. Even if she had been introduced to such views, she likely would have chosen to support her son fully. She reflected on the reasoning for this. In her family of origin, love was conditional, but her family would be different. Her parents divorced when she was quite young. Her mother was diagnosed with schizophrenia, and after a turbulent few years of attempting to manage her delusions and volcanic moods, Arianna and her sister, Betty, moved in with their dad and his new wife. In defiance of their father's wishes, Arianna's older sister decided, at age nineteen, to visit their biological mother. Their father reacted by disowning Betty, with no apparent second thoughts. Arianna could never do to her son what her father had done to her sister. To her, being loved unconditionally by one's parents was essential, for it allowed a child to gain confidence and take risks. She would always be there to support Derrick.

Her advice to other mothers of gay children: "Listen, get yourself out of the picture; it's not about you. You love that person; you might not like or understand what they're doing. Your children are not a possession. There are joys and sorrows with child rearing, and you have to let your children go. They follow their own path, not yours."

My Observations

Often lasting lessons come through hardship. Arianna learned about the dangers of conditional love as a young girl when her father disowned her sister because of a simple act of disobedience. His actions helped shape Arianna into the compassionate and supportive person she is today. She and her ex-husband, vowing not to force Derrick to choose between two divorced parents, maintained a friendly relationship up till his death. After he died, Arianna continued to include his second wife in family events.

The key to balance in Arianna's life is surrounding herself with a multitude of interests and people. She knows that while any stressor can seem momentarily overwhelming, its effect on her can be soft-ened by the love she gives and receives from others. Arianna is content in her own life. She knows she does not own her son, and fully accepts him and his partner.

Leslie

Leslie is the mother of two adult daughters from an early marriage. In her first ten years as a single mother she struggled financially, not expecting to be the single head of a household. She went on public assistance for a short time but soon found professional employment, where her talents were deeply valued by her employer. She has been with the same company for twenty years and has advanced from a clerical aide to a supervisory position.

After thirteen years of single parenthood, Leslie married her second husband, Richard. The two share a strong devotion to Catholicism, the religion in which Leslie raised her daughters. Leslie has dreamed that her children will marry and have children, but as we saw with Arianna, one's vision of the future is not immune to adaptation.

Several years ago Leslie's elder daughter, Ann-Marie, revealed herself to be a lesbian. While not totally surprised by this admission, Leslie has struggled with Ann-Marie's sexual preference. For one thing, Leslie believes that Ann-Marie chose the lesbian lifestyle prematurely, with-out giving heterosexual dating a chance. Beyond that, Leslie's inter-pretation of her faith understands homosexuality as a sinful act inconsistent with God's desire. In the face of these concerns, Leslie has sought out the advice of her parish priest, who has encouraged her to accept her daughter's sexuality: "Is it worth losing your daugh-ter? You want to keep the relationship, don't you?" When she left the church that day, Leslie was ready to turn her concerns over to God. "It's not for me to judge her. My job is to love her. I had to let go for my own peace of mind; it was out of my control. As much as we want our kids to be like us, they're not."

Leslie has worked at accepting her daughter's lifestyle. She has formed a relationship with Ann-Marie's partner, Marsha, whose own parents have had similar struggles coming to terms with the relation-ship. Leslie and Richard have had the young couple stay at their home and, gradually, Leslie has become more comfortable with their living together. Last Christmas, Ann-Marie and Marsha each invited their families to spend the holiday at the condo they share. Although not completely at ease with the arrangement, Leslie, Richard, and Leslie's other daughter celebrated the holiday at the condo.

Now Leslie is faced with another challenge—the young women are planning to get married. Both families, of course, have been invited to the ceremony and celebration. If the Christmas get-together was a milestone for the young women, their marriage will mark yet another step forward: the legitimization of their relationship through public disclosure that they are a couple. Leslie is having a very hard time with this: "I want my love to be unconditional, but maybe it is not," she told me. "You love your child so much and don't want to break her heart. But the reality is that I'm *going* to break it if I do not attend."

Leslie's hesitation to attend the wedding is not going over well with her daughter and her partner. And the issue goes beyond Leslie's showing up—Ann-Marie and Martha also hoped their parents would help pay for the wedding. It appears that will not happen. In Leslie's mind, her daughter should respect her non-involvement: "[She] wants me to respect her ideas and wishes, but it is a two-way street." When pressed, she admits the decision to attend or not will be a struggle till the very end. "It's a tricky balance—wanting to honor myself and love Ann-Marie."

Leslie's Observations

When I spoke with her last, Leslie told me she believed the wedding would not be the final hurdle for their families. Now Ann-Marie and Marsha are talking about having children. "It's not going to get easier. It will never be what the girls want it to be. There will always be another hurdle for everyone concerned. We just try to be accepting and loving."

Despite these challenges, Leslie is learning a great deal. She and Ann Marie have had their share of disagreements, but Leslie realizes that getting angry and using hateful words solves nothing and only makes the situation worse. Rather than forming hasty conclusions, she recommends that parents inform themselves about homosexuality and evaluate where their views derive from. "Before you have a dialogue, search your heart. Know what is bothering you and what is the core thing." In Leslie's mind, there is some choice in whether one acts upon his or her homosexual feelings, but she also understands that love looks different to everybody. As her daughter once said to her, "You don't always get to choose who you love."

"If I want to have a relationship with her, I have to keep an open mind and leave my judgments at the door. Those are the two most important things to remember. Also, have a support system. And as I said before, get educated. Homosexuality is not what people want to make it out to be."

My Observations

It is clear Leslie and her daughter love each other, and each values what the other thinks. Despite their differences, there is a deep connection they are committed to maintaining. Leslie is proud of her daughter on many levels. She believes she has raised Ann-Marie with a firm foundation in morality, good manners, and respect. She knows others recognize her daughter's character and talents. While they disagree on the matter of homosexuality—whether it is correctly understood as "choosing" a person, or a person "choosing homosexuality"—they continue to address their differences respectfully.

Leslie realizes her words mean a lot to Ann-Marie, that as a parent, "You have to be careful in your judgments, because parents still do have a lot of power." Yet what mother and daughter have in common—their commitment to their beliefs and values—is what also divides them. Hopefully, their love for each other will see them through this latest challenge. Leslie's love for her daughter will not be diminished, whether she attends the wedding or not; and Ann-Marie will not see this one event as the sole divining rod against which to judge her mother's love.

Lessons Learned

Life challenges us to accept its dialectics: we are faced with competing emotions and views, not easily reconciled. As part of our growth process, we must balance these sometimes oppositional parts of ourselves. Both Arianna and Leslie have talked at length with their children about their feelings and beliefs regarding sexual identity. This does not mean that they will reach mutual agreement. Sometimes the process goes on indefinitely, with no tidy resolution. Still, keeping respectful of your children's views is essential.

Perhaps because both women have rich lives themselves they do not have to focus exclusively on their children's sexual behavior. They recognize the boundaries between parent and child, and understand that their adult children's sexual preferences are more a matter of their children's concern than their own. Even accepting parents may still have their own discomfort and fears about revealing their children's sexual orientation with others. Here are a few additional thoughts:

1. Having a relationship with our children should always trump their sexual preference.

2. Your child's sexuality is about him or her, not you. It is your child's task to live his or her life authentically. Yours is to come to terms with who that person is.

3. Coming to terms with your child's sexuality does not necessarily come easily, nor does it always mean embracing his or her alternative lifestyle. Give yourself permission and time to explore what your child's orientation means to you. Get support from others if you are struggling.

4. When your adult child reveals his or her sexual identity, it may seem like a premature conclusion. Remember, your child likely has given it months or even years of thought. You will not convince your child it is just a phase he or she is going through.

5. Recognize how very hard it may be for your child to come forward with the announcement about his or her sexuality. It is a time for listening, not advice-giving.

6. You may be challenged to give up the dreams you had for your child; you may do some grieving. Look for blessings and new dreams that may come for both of you.

PART FOUR

Saving Yourself

- - - - - - - - - - - - - - - - - -

CHAPTER THIRTEEN

Their Pain is Our Pain

There may be no greater agony for parents than the experience of seeing a child in physical or emotional pain. But how should parents handle situations when they cannot provide a solution? Are there limits to empathy? Can we have too much empathy, to the point that it is harmful? Absolutely. The answer may seem counterintuitive, but it is no less true. Children do not want their parents to be derailed by their problems, and, as parents, we must understand where to draw the line between being compassionate caregivers and sacrificial lambs. In this chapter, we will look at our capacity to feel another's pain and how our life experiences color our responses to the struggles of our adult children.

Life Experiences

By the time children reach adulthood, most parents have lived four or more decades. With the passage of the innocence and naiveté of youth comes an awareness of the tribulations we may encounter as a result of our choices, as well as a recognition that factors outside of our control can drastically alter our life's plans. Parents have the wisdom to know that situations often resolve themselves over time. They have the depth of understanding to envision positive outcomes even when their children are stymied with doubt.

But there is something besides maturity at work here: Children of this generation live in a different era, an era of economic uncertainty and mobile career trajectories where the quest for financial stability takes time. Professional careers may have been more easily attainable and more durable for our generation when it was not uncommon for someone to take a job at a bank and work there for forty years. Now banks change hands just about every election cycle, and there is arguably less of a premium on training and keeping employees. When parents find their children steering away from traditional career choices or jumping from one job to the next parents can have "anticipatory" pain, what most of us know as anxiety. The protective parental instinct is to "save" or "rescue" our adult children, but this is often not in their best interest and might actually interfere with their ability to find their own solutions. It takes a certain amount of self-restraint to have empathy for a child's situation without becoming emotionally injured as a result.

In August 2011, thirty American military personnel, including twenty-two Navy Seal commandos, as well as eight Afghans, were killed when their Chinook transport helicopter was shot down west of Kabul, Afghanistan. The mother of any young woman who lost her husband in the incident has not just her own grief to deal with, but that of her daughter as well. She faces the dual tasks of supporting her daughter and processing her own emotions. If she is a caring mother, she will not want her daughter to put her own grief aside, yet she also must keep herself from tumbling into depression. Her situation exemplifies the challenge many of us face: empathizing with another without becoming dysfunctional ourselves; and, indeed, maintaining an appropriate level of empathy can be a tricky balance. In the next several pages, we'll take a look at exactly what empathy is, and how it can be both blessing and curse.

Empathy

Put simply, empathy is the ability to accurately perceive and understand another's emotions and experiences. This requires sensitivity, a capacity to put ourselves into another's "mental shoes."[1] According to the psychiatrist Pinchas Noy, a professor emeritus at Hebrew University, in Jerusalem, empathy is an emotional rather than an intellectual awareness of another person.[2] In addition to the capacity to feel another's pain, healthy empathy requires the ability to separate the self from the non-self, to have compassion for the victims of Hurricane Katrina without having lived through it ourselves.

Empathy is considered a prerequisite to moral behavior and can be viewed on a continuum. At one end are the psychopaths, individuals who may keenly perceive the emotions and experiences of others, but who nevertheless lack the capacity to identify or sympathize with those feelings. At the other end are those who would seem to have *too much* empathy. Being able to feel what another feels is a positive thing: a foundation for a moral society. But some people are so masterfully attuned to other's feelings and experiences, they feel overwhelmed any time another is in pain. These individuals, whom the psychiatrist Judith Orloff calls empaths, lack sufficient boundaries to separate themselves from another's suffering.

In her book *Emotional Freedom: Liberate Yourself From Negative Emotions and Transform Your Life*, Orloff describes empaths as "naturally giving, spiritually attuned and good listeners. If you want heart, empaths have got it."[3] She says that they absorb emotions of others, often to their detriment. They are more vulnerable to negativity and may develop panic attacks and depression, as well as other physical symptoms. Orloff believes that many people diagnosed with chronic fatigue syndrome—a complex disorder characterized by extreme lethargy, joint and muscle pain, and enlarged lymph nodes—are actually misdiagnosed empaths.

Similar to Orloff's empaths, the psychologist Elaine Aron, in her book *The Highly Sensitive Person: How to Thrive When the World Overwhelms You*,[4] writes about "highly sensitive people" (HSP), those easily aroused and vulnerable to slight changes in their environment. Their traits include being conscientious, being easily moved by music and the arts, getting rattled by having a lot to do in a short amount of time, withdrawing from high levels of stimulation and noise, and avoiding violent movies or media. People who are HSPs are highly reactive to change and "deeply affected by other people's moods and emotions."[5] They may find much in common with empaths; however not all HSPs are empaths. Both are sensitive to crowds, their environment, overstimulation, and the moods of others. But empaths take their sensitivity to another level. They cannot separate others' pain from their own. They can't *not* feel for another; their empathy, while at times a gift, can be debilitating.

Let's take a look at one classic case of empathy gone too far.

Olivia

Olivia, a health and wellness counselor at a major teaching hospital, is married with two adult children. Both children live and work on the West Coast, as do Olivia and her husband. Olivia, a self-described empath, is well aware of her extreme sensitivity and describes her empathy as pathological. She says, "I have the same reaction to large and small events, in which a person or animal is in distress. I get sick to my stomach, light-headed. I feel weak and cry. It's like I get into their heads. Whatever is happening to them is happening to me." She recalls seeing an orphaned fawn trying to nurse from his dead mother's body after the mother had been hit by a car, not far from her house. She felt as though the fawn were her own child. After bringing the infant deer home, she purchased an appropriate formula and bottle fed him until he could go off on its own.

For much of her life, Olivia thought this kind of behavior was normal; that everyone shared her deeply felt concern for animals and people. When she learned that was not true, that her empathy was exceptional, the knowledge was quite a revelation. It caused her to consider how her health and well-being were being affected. After visiting a number of professionals, she learned her hyper-vigilance to the inner thoughts and feelings of others has compromised her immune system and contributed to her diagnosis of chronic fatigue syndrome.

Olivia's unlimited store of empathy can be especially problematic in the context of childrearing. When Olivia's adult son and his longtime girlfriend broke up, she was hit so hard by the news she spent three days in bed, despairing, unable to walk. In order to construct a boundary, her psychiatrist cautioned her against answering the phone, but Olivia simply could not do this. She lost weight and had a breakdown herself. "Everything they suffered, I suffered. It was like being gutted with a knife." One year later, thinking about the breakup still causes her tremendous emotional pain: "Like processing a morbid death . . . That's absurd. Others move on. I just cannot *not* be there for people."

Olivia's extreme sensitivity and health problems led her to the study of complementary and holistic medicines and her current professional practice. Ironically, when she is working with seriously ill people in a medical setting, Olivia feels the most calm and grounded: "With the gravely ill, I can move out of myself." She has come up with her own coping strategies—calming hobbies such as writing poetry, reading scripture, listening to relaxing music.

Orloff and Aaron have other suggestions for their readers. First, be self-aware: know what triggering situations may cause overstimulation, as well as those that are calming, so that you balance activity with quiet socialization and privacy. By doing a little advance planning, a sensitive person can anticipate potential problems and develop back-up plans—for instance, making arrangements to leave a boisterous event early, if she knows she will reach her limit before her friends do.

Parents' personal histories as well as their temperament affect how they experience empathy. It is natural at times to project one's own feelings onto our children. Parents should not assume, however, their adult children are having the same feelings as they had in similar situations. A woman from an abusive family, for example, will be well tuned-in to signs of abuse. If she suspects her daughter is in an abusive relationship, she will be able to feel her daughter's pain at a deeper level than she would had she not been abused herself.

Identifying the presence or absence of empathy in another is not easy. The woman who had to be "tough" to survive a chaotic marriage may hide her empathic feelings beneath an armor of disaffection and detachment. Her adult children, when in crisis, may mistake her demeanor as insensitive or unfeeling. The truth is that to keep from being overwhelmed she blocks her true feelings from expression. This is generally not done at a conscious level.

Women's Edge in Handling Stress?

For many years now, scientists have known that a stress response, called the "fight-or-flight syndrome" is built into human DNA. Adrenaline increases when we feel a threat to ourselves or our loved ones, and we become biologically poised to physically struggle or to flee the situation. Although men and women have been known to handle stress differently, new evidence is emerging that some of the differences are hard-wired.

Recently, Shelley Taylor and her colleagues at the University of California, Los Angeles, proposed that the stress-fighting arsenal of women reflects a pattern of "tend and befriend."[6] Tending refers to how females nurture their offspring to protect their young from danger and to keep the young calm. Befriending refers to female habits of social bonding, which usually lead women to talk with other women when under stress. According to Taylor, women are much more likely than men to seek the support of friends in stressful situations, including those involving relationship problems, health complications, or work conflicts.

One explanation for their dissimilar responses to stress is that men and women release different levels of hormones when under stress. Males tend to release more testosterone, which provides the impetus for the "fight-or-flight" reaction, whereas women release greater amounts of the hormone oxytocin, which increases relaxation and reduces the body's stress response. Some researchers believe oxytocin actually counters the physiological effects of stress on the system and produces a protective effect. When in the tending mode, women benefit hormonally, but so do their offspring: touch and massage enhance an infant's immune system, decrease pain, and ensure normal growth.

The tendency for women to befriend when under stress is seen across the life span. From adolescence to adulthood, females seek out more same-sex support than their male counterparts. This is one of the most pronounced differences between the sexes—women interact with each other more frequently and on a wider variety of issues than men. As a result, their nervous systems are generally calmer and they have a better ability to recover from the physiological effects of acute stress. More research is being done to explore this topic and determine if there is more flexibility in the male stress response than previously thought.

Implications for You as a Parent

Parents undoubtedly feel the suffering of their children. Confronted with their children's grief and pain, they have to decide when to take direct action, when to walk beside their children, and when to step aside. Intuition, prior experience, and developmental research may all help guide this process. Ultimately, what actions a parent takes, and what she gleans from them involves a deeply personal understanding of her child and herself as individuals. To return to the dance of differentiation metaphor, a good dancer understands the abilities and limitations of her partner, but she also understands her own limits—one can only stretch and bend so far before risking a fall.

Your child's temperament may test your parenting style. A hands-on parent might have to learn to cope with the expectations of an adult child who does not want or need such involved assistance. The reverse might also be true: a child may want his parents to rescue him well into his adult years, while his parents know this is a recipe for trouble. You may simply want to take some time for yourself to do something enjoyable—ride a bike, take a trip to the lake, visit Las Vegas—without having to be continuously emotionally available for your child. All of these reactions are normal. Just as a cell phone or an iPad needs recharging, so does a person. You will not be a valuable resource to your child if you are completely worn out.

Recognizing and respecting your own emotional and financial limitations is not easy. A good rule of thumb is this: If your functioning at work or in your relationships is suffering, then you are nearing your emotional limit. In such cases, talking to others to get additional perspectives is helpful. Remember you are not being lazy or unproductive when you relax—you are charging your inner battery. If the relationship you have with your children is not going to change significantly or at all, you must find ways to achieve peace for yourself.

- - - - - - - - - - - - - - - - - - - -

CHAPTER FOURTEEN

Grief and Loss

We grieve losses large and small. From the sadness we feel when a work confidant leaves for employment elsewhere, to the more serious loss of financial security or the devastating loss of a child, none of us is immune to grief. A parent's grief need not arise from as serious a loss as death to be significant. A child may be sent to a foreign country to engage in military service or decide to join the Peace Corps to fight the spread of infectious diseases. More severe are circumstances that trigger grief through a metaphoric death: parent-child relationships severed beyond repair; adult children who suffer from debilitating physical or mental illness or who choose a lifestyle of substance addiction or crime. Any of these can be cause for tremendous anguish.

Here we'll explore the devastating circumstances all parents dread and some have to endure—which may or may not involve the actual death of a child. We'll consider the dynamics that accompany parents' phases of grieving and discuss ways of coping. Rather than looking at grief as something to be avoided, we'll take the approach that grief is a series of emotions we may experience and pass through in a healthy way, and that by enduring grief we deepen our faith in our ability to persevere.

Losing an Adult Child

The death of a child is a devastating event for any parent. We expect to watch our children grow into adulthood and have families of their own. To outlive a child defies all natural expectations. According to the Compassionate Friends,[1] a national organization that helps families who have lost children, an adult child's death has some unique aspects. For one thing, the grief of surviving parents is often minimized with prosaic comments: "You should be thankful your daughter lived as long as she did. You had her throughout her childhood."[2] This reasoning obviously offers little consolation. Additionally, parents have lost more than just their child. As relationships often deepen over the years, they may have lost a good friend as well. They feel abandoned, scared, and lonely. On top of all that, they feel tremendous guilt.

When we become parents, we take on the most important role in our lives. Caring for our offspring is built into our biology. If something happens to our children, we cannot help but think that we have failed in that most primal obligation: their protection. It doesn't matter if they are five or fifty. Their well-being is always seen as our responsibility at some level, and particularly when we are under duress, at which point rationality gives way to basic emotions—despair and guilt.

Guilt comes in many forms. Parents may feel guilty for outliving the child or for not being able to save the child from death. If the child's death was the result of suicide, serious mental illness, or substance abuse parents often blame themselves for not having intervened enough or sooner. Of course we all know that we cannot live another adult's life for her. We cannot force our children into treatment, and we certainly cannot force them to be happy. Otherwise well-adjusted families can have an adult child whose life has been one struggle after the next. No amount of time or money can guarantee that one's son or daughter will survive and thrive. This is a heartbreaking revelation for many parents.

One of the byproducts of the death of a child is the significant impact the loss may have on the parents' relationships with their other children. Parents and children are naturally at different life stages. While the death of a sibling is undoubtedly high on the list of life-changing events that an adult child may experience, there is no guarantee it will prompt surviving children to express their grief in a way that is obvious to parents. Children may hold back their own emotions to protect their parents, or immerse themselves in the task of planning for the future to avoid facing the pain of bereavement. Parents can misread these actions and believe their children are not sufficiently mourning the loss, when, in fact, they are expressing their grief adequately, if abstractly. If attuned to the signals, parents will find their adult children are often highly capable of processing their own grief and may even, when appropriate, give their parents the message that they need to move on.

For many parents, the passing of a child means a radically altered vision of the future. Rather than looking forward to events in life, they are compelled to look back. There is the longing to see and touch their child one more time, the fear that as time goes by they will forget what their child looked like. Some parents feel physical pain. Others wish to join their child beyond the grave, as life, it seems, has lost meaning. It is not uncommon for parents to be afraid to allow themselves to live happily again, as if they are undeserving of peace or joy. Sadly, for many parents, the capacity to experience joy feels gone forever. It is important to keep in mind that as painful as grief can seem in the first months and years after the loss of a child, its edges will soften with time.

Spousal relationships are affected by loss as well. While it is true that an adult child's death often puts a strain on her parents' marriage, the actual number of marriages ending in divorce following a child's death is somewhat low: only about 12 percent, according to results obtained from a 1999 survey of bereaved parents.[3] These results were confirmed in a 2006 survey, which showed only a slightly higher divorce rate of bereaved parents: 16 percent.[4] Responding appropriately to your partner during this time requires an adequate understanding of gender dynamics. Men and women are known to grieve differently, with women typically being more expressive of their emotions and grief, and men showing more reserve. In a scenario the late Jeanne Webster Blank, author of *The Death of an Adult Child* describes—which I've witnessed in my office—a bereaved wife pours forth her anguish, not really in a conversation with anyone.[5] Her husband, unable to fix things for her, feels like a failure, to the point where all he can do is withdraw. His wife feels left alone with her distress, interprets his withdrawal as anger and insensitivity, and gets even more distressed. It sets up a "perfect storm" for a widening rift.

That parents of adult children are often empty nesters adds to the severity of their experience of loss. Unless grandchildren are present, Blank argues, the emptiness of the house takes on heightened significance and comes to symbolize the child's absence. Even parents highly attuned to their spouses will have to defend themselves against feelings of alienation from each other, and the rest of the world.

Stages of Grieving

Elisabeth Kübler-Ross and David Kessler take the stages of grieving identified in Kübler-Ross's seminal work, *On Death and Dying*,[6] and apply them to the loss of a loved one in *On Grief and Grieving*.[7] Identifying denial, anger, bargaining, depression, and acceptance as grief's five stages, the authors show how grief is experienced by individuals in a complex but recognizable sequence of emotions. In *The Death of an Adult Child* Blank adapts Kübler-Ross's stages of grieving to the unique experience of parents suffering the loss an adult child:[8]

Phase 1: Shock, Numbness, and Denial. Initial shock that their adult child has died; difficulty accepting that they will not see him again.

Phase 2: Anger and Guilt. Anger at self, their child, and others for their loss; extreme guilt.

Phase 3: Acute Phase. Intense sadness and depression, often accompanied by erratic behavior, physical illness, yearning and searching, withdrawal from others.

Phase 4: Reality and Acceptance. Internalization of the fact that their adult child is forever gone; beginnings of reintegration of their lives with renewed purpose.

During the first phase of grief, typically the shortest, parents are preoccupied with the immediate details a death necessitates, such as funeral preparations, the settling of assets, and the difficult task of communicating the news of the death to relatives. The shock and numbness immediately following the death of a child are likely to evolve into hotter, more palpable emotions as the reality of death sets in. Blank notes, however, that those parents of an adult child living away from home at the time of her death are prone to get stuck in the first stage of denial for quite some time. Since the child was not a daily presence in their lives before her death, parents have an easier time denying it: "Jackie will be coming home from college. She is just gone for awhile." If these thoughts persist, they are a cause for concern as they may keep parents from moving through the other phases of grief.

Experiencing the guilt of the second phase is normal for parents who lose an adult child. Because parents almost universally feel tremendous responsibility for their children, being realistic about the nature and severity of their guilt can be daunting. Many parents contemplate what they could or should have done, and how, at some level, they feel culpable for their child's fate. It is far too easy for parents to find reasons to berate themselves for past actions: "If only I hadn't worked when she was in middle school—then she would never have tried drugs; she'd probably be alive today." The better route is to explore the motivating forces underlying the guilt and evaluate the situation dispassionately: "I want so badly to make sense of what happened that I'm looking for any and all connections between what I did and what happened. The truth is there are lots of middle school kids who try drugs, whether their parents work or not. It's hard to accept that I was unable to protect her from making choices that would hurt her."

Guilt that accompanies the second phase can appear repeatedly, often as anger directed at everyday events, God, doctors, and so on. For example, a parent whose daughter died in a friend's car may feel anger at the surviving friend, at the girl's parents who loaned her their car; at God for "taking away" their daughter; and even at the daughter for riding with a drunk or inexperienced driver. They may cut off contact with the friend and her family. They may drop out of their church because a "loving God would not have taken Sara." They may spend hours poring through documents about the safety record of the make and model of car and consider suing the auto manufacturer. All these are efforts to assign blame *somewhere*. Being angry is a distraction that, for a while, keeps them from the Acute Phase, in which they're likely to experience intense feelings of emptiness and despair.

And indeed, the Acute Phase is often the most difficult. According to Blank, "This wretched stage builds during the first year and often reaches its peak during the second year after the child's death."[9] Most parents manage to get through the first year, including difficult occasions such as birthdays and anniversaries, despite incredible pain. The second year brings the expectation for parents that they will feel better, but often that is not the case. It is during this second year that some parents begin to engage in risky behavior, such as using alcohol and drugs, overspending, overworking, overeating, or withdrawing from the company of their friends. Too often the temptation is for parents to give up on caring for themselves, and sadly it is these parents who are at the greatest risk for suicide. Confronting deep pain means allowing oneself to experience sadness, not avoid it. But many individuals have difficulty doing this on their own. Family and friends, counseling and support groups, and prescription drug treatments can help individuals manage their lives during this difficult stage.

There is no precise timetable to mark the phases of grief, but at some point most parents have the realization that their lives, although changed, will continue. In this fourth phase, the task for parents is to regain their physical and mental health and restructure their lives. Ideally, in facing a future without the child, parents will bring their insights and altered life perspectives to bear as they create a new normal for themselves. While the pain of the loss will still be there, it will no longer take center stage. Reaching this final phase may take years. As Blank puts it, "acceptance" does not mean accepting a child's death but the reality and finality of the loss.

Acceptance will assume varied forms. Some parents will move to a new city or downsize to a smaller home. Others will renew old interests such as gardening or playing the piano. In many cases, new interests emerge; these endeavors are particularly significant when a parent knows they would have pleased her deceased child. Some parents put their energy into helping others who have gone through the same crises, or helping animals. There are as many ways to move forward as there are parents able to do so.

From what I have heard from parents and gathered in my readings about them, theirs is a life perspective forever altered: it is sobered, wizened, and intolerant of pettiness. While they know they cannot escape the pain of loss altogether, they are still capable of enjoying life's pleasures. They have come to terms with the death of their loved one and found in their daily activities ways to remember and honor her.

Estrangement and Incarceration

Long-term or permanent estrangement from an adult child is a severe loss with its own dynamics, and we can apply the phases of grieving to this kind of loss as well. When parents are blindsided by an adult child's withdrawal from them, they often go into a kind of shock. Refusing to believe the separation has occurred, they will contact their child repeatedly, trying to figure out what has happened. Frequently, they find themselves apologizing and making egregious accommodations—willing to do almost anything to make things right. When their efforts fall short, parents become angry with their child and, at times, with each other. Estrangement is especially difficult when the adult child singles his parents out for ostracism while maintaining contact with other family members. As the child tries to get his relatives to "side" with him, both the immediate and extended family are put in an uncomfortable position.

Depression on the parent's part usually accompanies an estrangement in which the child shows no willingness to reconcile. Parents yearn for the relationship they once had and live in a state of semi-confusion, continuing to try to make sense of what has occurred. Similar to losses involving death, the grief of estrangement can be potent at holidays, birthdays, and other major events, when the absence of the family member is readily apparent. Hostile responses—or worse yet, no response at all from an estranged child—are additional blows that may feed a parent's depression and lower his self-worth.

During this period, parents often seek the help of counselors; however, therapy may not always yield the desired result of reunification. Therapists may try to get the estranged family members together to discuss the situation, but the only willing participants may be the parents themselves. Parents may be left with only one choice: to find a way to accept an altered vision of their family. Just as in situations where a death has occurred, estranged parents must discover new avenues to reinforce their worth and give their lives meaning again. It is not that the pain of their loss leaves them as they take on new pursuits, but that it becomes more tolerable and no longer dominates their lives.

Parents of adult children who have been incarcerated also deal with tremendous grief, not only because of the absence of their child from their lives, but also due to the shameful circumstances of the child's imprisonment. Friends and family members are often reluctant to inquire as to the well-being of the adult child, or to even mention his name. "It is as if he doesn't even exist anymore," one mother said. "My family is careful *not* to talk about him."

In many of these cases, the child's pattern of antisocial behavior began long ago. The initial shock or denial a parent feels on account of a child's actions will eventually give way to feelings of anger and guilt. Parents may be angry with many different people: their child, the system, the child's peer group, other parents, and so on. The circumstances of a child's prison sentence is not something that parents are likely to share at the water cooler or over coffee, and many parents withdraw from colleagues and friends.

Much like bereaved parents, those who have a son or daughter in prison have had to let go of the dream of how they expected their child's life to be. Conflicting emotions rage within—sorrow, anger, love, hopelessness. Often there is the hope that the child's life will be different upon release. If it is not, the parent must endure yet another blow to her psyche. As a therapist, I have been consistently impressed with the fortitude of mothers whose children have been incarcerated: women who drive for hours to visit their son or daughter for only a few minutes; women who take their grandchildren to see their incarcerated father, or provide a home and support to a son's spouse and children during his imprisonment. It is through acts of kindness and generosity like these that many parents find renewed purpose in their own lives.

Thankfully, there are resources for mothers who have a child in prison. One such support group is Mothers of Incarcerated Sons Society (M.I.S.S.).[10] Their current project is to persuade legislators to change the laws regarding how the mentally ill are processed in the judicial system. Among their concerns is the lack of long-term residential treatment for the mentally ill once they have been released from prison. The scarcity of housing and programs increases the vulnerability of these individuals to chronic homelessness, as well the likelihood of repeating illegal behaviors in an effort to self-medicate or find shelter. Another resource is PrisonTalk.com, a forum for families with a loved one in prison which addresses general questions about the legal system, as well as specific issues such as domestic violence and immigration concerns.[11] PrisonTalk also hosts blogs for parents of prisoners. These special "sororities" provide an atmosphere of comfort and empathy, in which families can engage in meaningful dialogue about the difficult issues they face.

Anticipatory Grief

The parent of an adult child with a terminal illness may experience grieving in anticipation of the coming loss. Kübler-Ross and Kessler address this in *On Grief and Grieving*. Just as in grief after the death of a loved one, the way that anticipatory grief is experienced is unique to the individual, and can include the five stages of loss. "Anticipatory grief is the 'beginning of the end' in our minds," the authors write. "We now operate in two worlds, the safe world that we are used to and the unsafe world in which a loved one might die."[12] And while such grief may help an individual prepare for what is coming, it does not replace the grief that comes after a death. Parents should recognize this process as normal and, while not ignoring it, try to maintain their regular activities. They can also seek out comfort by talking with others. Depending on the type and length of the illness, anticipatory grief can last from weeks to years.

Any parent whose child cannot or chooses not to function productively in our society may be thrust into an anticipatory grieving mode as well. This is especially true for those whose adult children are involved in illegal activities or live on the streets. I've spoken with several women who've told me that each day they await a call from the police, bearing the sad news their child is dead. Some say the only way they can prevent themselves from suffering is to expect the worst— that way their dreams for their children are not consistently dashed. In fact, some mothers who experience anticipatory grief admit that it might be easier if their children were dead, so they wouldn't have to experience the continual pain of uncertainty.

Mothers of adult children with serious problems live between two worlds: one, the world with which most of us are familiar, in which people get up, go to work and meet their daily obligations; and two, the world with which we want no association, where parents acquire the vocabulary of bail bonds and the penal system, of detox and drug treatment facilities, of half-way houses and long-term psychiatric facilities.

Claim Your Peace

Regardless of the reason for their grief, many parents have found ways to recharge themselves and claim their peace. Here are a few lessons worth noting:

1. *Don't wait to get out of your rut and do something to help yourself.* That's not how recovery works. Even if you join an activity half-heartedly, you may find that you are able to enjoy yourself.

2. *Be with people who are understanding.* Take advantage of support groups in your area and online. Local hospitals frequently are excellent resources. Share confidences. You don't have to answer every question put to you, just those you are comfortable with.

3. *Don't try to get through the grieving process alone.* Our bodies and minds are designed to benefit from connecting with others. Being in the company of others will help you recover physically and emotionally.

4. *Take care of yourself.* Exhaustion will leave you incapable of developing existing relationships in your life. Self-martyrdom doesn't work; it just turns others away.

5. *Allow the grieving process to unfold, stage by stage.* This will look and feel different for each person.

6. *Resist the urge to accuse yourself of backsliding if you bounce back and forth between the stages.* Remember, these are only a framework for consideration as you grieve. There is no single destination or arrival time.

7. *Don't give up on intimate contact.* When you are struggling is when you may need such contact the most. Physical affection and sex with your partner can be grounding and bring you into the present. These are moments of peace worth claiming.

- - - - - - - - - - - - - - - - - -

CHAPTER FIFTEEN

Forgiveness and Letting Go

For a generation that has been highly capable of pleasing others to achieve success, our instincts lead us to want to fix the hurts and right the wrongs. But we find that we are sometimes helpless to change situations to our liking. We may use all of our problem-solving and relationship building skills to no avail. In this chapter, we explore the challenges of letting go of expectations and attachments and learning to forgive. These can be tremendously difficult tasks, but in some situations they may be the only way to achieve inner peace.

Most people hold strong opinions about forgiveness. Usually rooted in childhood experiences, these views reflect how forgiveness was practiced in our homes and religious institutions. "Say you're sorry" is a refrain many of us heard growing up and may have used with our own children. That simple directive is loaded with questions: If you are not truly sorry, is it right to say it? Does saying "I'm sorry" let you off the hook? What about the receiver of the apology? What if she is still hurt and angry? What about her feelings? On the other hand, if you are the one who desires forgiveness, can you have peace if another refuses to make amends?

As in other difficult relationships, a strained relationship between a parent and her adult child will not automatically end with a pure and gracious act of forgiveness. There are variations as to how forgiveness is given and accepted. You may be quick to forgive and have a child who holds grudges. Or you may be the grudge-holder with a child who wants to move on, forgive and forget. A person's ability to forgive is influenced by her temperament and the extent of the perceived hurt.

Heinous acts such as murder are extremely difficult, if not impossible, for some to forgive. And perhaps rightly so.

Since there are multiple ways of looking at forgiveness, let's start with a clear description of what it is *not*. The list below is derived from my thoughts and the work of Fred Luskin and Robert Enright who have written previously on the subject.[1]

1. *Forgiving does not mean forgetting what has occurred.* We may learn to let go of pain, but we are not likely to forget it. Nor would it be wise to forget it, as we might find ourselves returning to risky and harmful situations—continuing to trust a daughter who promises to repay money loaned to her, but never does.

2. *Forgiving does not mean you tolerate, excuse, or overlook the actions that have been hurtful.* The idea of forgiving has too often been equated with excusing the actions of the hurtful person. When our children were small, we forgave them many times. Still, we held them accountable. That is how people learn and how we behave as a just society. At the adult level, a mother may forgive her twenty-five-year-old son for stealing from her, but require him to relinquish his keys to her home and car so that he no longer has access to her belongings.

3. *Forgiving does not mean that you should ignore your feelings or try to minimize them.* Denying your feelings will only make forgiving more difficult. If people are quick to brush aside their anger, hurt, and disappointment, these feelings can sink underground and contribute to resentment and other adverse emotional and physical consequences. It is healthier to acknowledge and recognize your feelings, so that you can begin to address them.

4. *Forgiving does not mean opening yourself to more abuse.* Far too many people think that forgiving someone gives that person an opening to continue abusive behavior. In fact, the opposite is true: not forgiving allows the abuse to continue psychologically. Re-experiencing the hurtful behavior again and again, one continues to suffer as if the events were still occurring.

5. *Forgiving does not mean that you and the other person will or should reconcile.* Forgiving increases the possibility for reconciliation, but does not guarantee it. A mother may forgive a son's hateful behaviors, yet choose to minimize or cease contact with him in order to protect herself in the future.

6. *Forgiving does not require a religious orientation.* Much of the writing on forgiveness occurs in a religious context. This is handy for the devout but may be frustrating for atheists and other non-believers. Fortunately, researchers such as Fred Luskin have developed models of forgiving that do not require one to hold particular religious beliefs.

7. *Forgiving is not a simple, one-step process.* If it were, it would be easy. Learning to forgive can be a difficult, if not impossible, task for some people.

8. *Forgiving is not something you do just for the other person.* While extending forgiveness does benefit the other person, you do it primarily for yourself. Most people who have been struggling for months or years with resentment eventually work to open themselves to forgiveness so they will heal.

What Is Forgiveness?

Forgiveness is an active experience. It happens when one confronts her pain completely, looks at the situation in new ways, and begins to take charge of her future well-being. Forgiveness does not always involve an increase in compassion for the offending party, but the forgiver will at least be released from resentment and hurt. As Luskin, former director of the Stanford University Forgiveness Project, says, "Forgiveness means that even though you are wounded you choose to hurt and suffer less."[2]

Forgiveness may or may not involve direct contact with the person you forgive—it is often an internal experience in which the forgiver lets go of the anger, resentment, hurt, and disappointment that have been plaguing her. You can forgive people with whom you have no contact, including those who have died.

Why Bother to Forgive?

Earlier in the book I spoke of parents being able to "claim their peace." That is why forgiveness is so important. Parents cannot have inner peace if they continue to struggle with the turmoil of uncontrollable events from their past. The initial response to being hurt or emotionally injured may be anger, but that anger should have an expiration date; left unresolved, it can poison our relationships and well-being.

One of the pioneers in the study of forgiveness, psychologist Robert Enright, distinguishes between anger and unresolved resentment. He says that anger "is the primary and in many ways proper response to injury." Resentment, however, "involves re-feeling the original anger. We remember the injury and re-feel the emotions . . . Anger is like a flame, resentment like a hot coal."[3]

Resentment is not to be taken lightly. Studies from as early as 1939 indicate a link between deep passive anger and physical symptoms such as high blood pressure.[4] Luskin cites studies at the University of Wisconsin which show that the more individuals are able to forgive, the fewer heart problems they report.[5] And not only can unresolved anger affect one's physical and emotional well-being, but it also may influence relationships with others in one's life. A mother estranged for years from her adult daughter may find that her relationship with her spouse is injured by the stress. She may withdraw from others or self-medicate to help herself cope. Her marriage can be jeopardized. And of course, the person who is the subject of resentment is also affected.

Lewis B. Smedes, author of *The Art of Forgiving*, says victims of hurt move through three stages of "unfair pain."[6] First is the "original wallop"— the incident that hurts someone to begin with: a daughter inexplicably rages at her parents, rattling off a litany of their inadequacies just after they paid her rent. Second, people remember how they were wronged or mistreated: the same daughter shows up for Sunday dinner acting as if nothing had happened, while her parents are still reeling from her incendiary outburst. Third, they may wish for equal pain for the perpetrator: the parents secretly hope their daughter suffers as much disrespect when her own children grow up.

In the last phase, resentment simmers at a low boil, awaiting an unwelcome event to set it ablaze. The offender may have moved on, but the hurt person keeps suffering. Reconciliation may or may not come with forgiveness, but there is absolutely no chance of repairing the relationship if resentment continues. By forgiving, we at least open the door to the possibility of reconciliation. As Smedes says, "When we forgive, we set a prisoner free and discover that the prisoner we set free is ourselves."[7]

Obstacles to Forgiving

In her compelling book *Toxic Parents: Overcoming their Hurtful Legacy and Reclaiming Your Life*,[8] Susan Forward helps her readers address pain inflicted by their parents. By her definition, forgiving implies overlooking wrongs. Other authors might disagree—arguing that confronting pain and anger is essential to forgiving, that forgiveness does not mean disregarding the past. For Forward, though, forgiveness is earned. What if the offending person never "earns" forgiveness, but continues to act in a vicious or hurtful manner? Should we be prisoners of their actions forever? No. We have permission, Forward says, not to forgive.

Understanding you have the right *not* to forgive can be the first step in allowing yourself to do so. To declare, "I forgive my daughter," while in the midst of resentment and hurt won't work, nor is it appropriate. Telling yourself or a friend he should forgive before he is ready may do more harm than good. It denies the reality of what has occurred and leaves the hurt person feeling stuck with his feelings, while perhaps adding guilt to the mix. The better choice is to acknowledge your feelings or those of your hurt friend. You can say to him, "I see you are really suffering. It may seem like you won't ever feel better, but there are some things you can do that might help."

Forgiving, in short, does not require an individual to develop positive feelings for the offender. That may never happen. It just means finding a way to be free of the toxicity of your negative thoughts and feelings, to disengage from resentments. Consider forgiving if you are experiencing some or all of the following:

1. Depression, anxiety, helplessness, hopelessness over a past hurt or disappointment

2. Feeling powerless in your life or lacking a sense of control

3. Inability to imagine a future emotionally "free" of the other person's actions

4. Anger and resentment that plays over and over in your mind

5. Repetitive fantasies of "getting even" with the other person

6. The ability to get extremely upset just thinking about the person and event

7. Altered relationships

8. Altered physical health

People who harbor feelings of resentment and hurt are stuck. Their attachment to their pain keeps them from living fully in the present and planning for the future. Left unaddressed this kind of paralysis can have long-term ramifications. People become prisoners of their thoughts and feelings. They continue to relive painful events as though they were happening in the present.

Considerable research is being conducted regarding the degree to which we can "rewire" or change the brain. Proponents of the brain's so-called "elasticity" say that by changing what it is we think about and concentrate on, we can literally change our brain. EMDR—Eye Movement Desensitization and Reprocessing Therapy—is an example of a relatively new treatment method believed to affect how the brain processes information. The theory behind this treatment—often used with people who suffer from Post Traumatic Stress Disorder (PTSD)—is that pathology may result from maladaptive encoding of adverse life experiences. Proponents claim that while EMDR doesn't make someone forget past events, it does remove the traumatic re-experiencing of the event. Symptoms are alleviated, distress is reduced or eliminated, and the brain is able to return to processing information and events normally.

Components of Forgiving

Learning new ways to process our experiences is essential to developing the ability to forgive. Below are a few strategies to help free yourself from the emotional strain of resentment:

1. Face the Hurt and Anger

- Do not rush to forgive. Forgiving before you are ready won't work.
- Take ownership that you have been hurt or wronged. Instead of minimizing your feelings, identify and express them fully—to yourself and someone you can trust.

- Be very clear about the particular event you have difficulty forgiving or letting go.

2. Face the Barriers

- Identify what keeps you from forgiving the person.

- Remember what forgiving is *not*—forgetting the offense or putting complete trust in that person again.

3. Visualize an Improved Life

- Picture yourself free of hurt and anger. Just visualizing inner peace may lower your blood pressure.[9]

4. Reframe Your View of the Offending Person

- Look at the offending person from a new angle. Viewing that person, not as a villain, but a flawed person with unique problems may make their offense feel less malicious.

- Ask yourself if the person is worthy of your energy and time. Consider what you could do with the additional time in your day.

5. Write Letters (You Don't Have to Send Them)

- Write a letter to the object of your resentment. Describe how you were wronged, your feelings, and your struggle to let go. Keep in mind that communicating to the person you are trying to forgive is not always necessary or wise. The goal is the frank expression of your thoughts and feelings.

- Write a letter to yourself if your feelings are changing and you find yourself beginning to let go. Describe how you are reclaiming your life. If you are still struggling, write about that.

6. *Rehearse New Behaviors*

- Practice living a few hours at a time as if you had let go of your resentment.

- Put your energies into activities and relationships that you find nourishing and rewarding.

- Take charge of your life. Becoming assertive is one of the best antidotes to feeling victimized. If you need help being assertive, find a good therapist, book, or group.

7. *Get Philosophical*

- Recognize that we cannot go through life without being hurt.

- Being a good, decent person provides no guarantee someone else will regard us that way.

PART FIVE

Going on From Here

CHAPTER SIXTEEN

Creating Drive

How Do You Do It?

For most parents there is the assumption and expectation that their children will surpass their achievements and aspire to even greater accomplishments. What happens, though, when your adult child does not share your motivation? Can parents actually create drive in their adult children? What defines the adult learner? And how do you help your adult child make a personal plan for success?

Accumulating evidence suggests that multiple nonheritable factors influence how someone develops and the level of determination he possesses to succeeed. David Shenk, in his book *The Genius in All of Us*, explains that genes do not directly cause personality traits, but rather from the moment of conception there is a "dynamic process of gene-environment interaction."[1] People are not born with musical talent, or math talent, per se. Rather their inherent traits are influenced and mediated by the environment. Genes "influence everything but strictly determine very little," according to Shenk.[2] A determinist might take exception to this view, citing the example of "savants"—people who, though verbally noncommunicative, possess mastery of an instrument. Shenk disagrees. The extraordinary talent we find in savants, he argues, is due to damage or abnormality in some part of their brains. Even for a genius, such as Mozart, there is a distinct link between "giftedness" and the enormous exposure and time devoted to cultivating this gift.

Mozart's father was a musician who focused intensely on the enrichment of his children's musical skills. When he realized that

Wolfgang, as a toddler, had more interest and potential than his older sister, he turned his efforts toward his son. The entire family put their stock in Mozart's future success from the age of three. It was not a simple matter of his being born with a musical gift.

Mozart's genius, of course, is only a sidebar to the much larger question of how people become motivated. The late twentieth century was witness to the "self-esteem movement," whose core theory held that children would thrive when their accomplishments were reinforced. Children who were frequently commended and told they were special and distinctive would excel in school and throughout their lives. Since then, several studies have challenged the value of unearned praise, suggesting that praise without accountability does nothing to encourage motivation and, in fact, may do just the opposite.[3]

Carol Dweck, a Stanford psychologist, found that children who were praised for their inborn intelligence were less likely to risk challenging tasks than those praised for being hard workers.[4] As part of her study, she and her research team assigned four hundred seventh grade students rather easy puzzles to complete. Afterwards she broke the students into two groups, telling one group they "must be smart at this," while telling the other they "must have really worked hard."[5] Then she offered the students an opportunity to try either another easy puzzle or a more challenging one. Interestingly, more than half of the students praised for being smart chose the easy puzzle. By contrast, ninety percent of the students praised for being hard workers chose the more difficult puzzle. Dweck concluded from this and other studies that those who believe in "inborn intelligence and talents are less intellectually adventurous and less successful in school" than those who believe intelligence can be increased with effort.[6]

David Shenk, writing about Carol Dweck and others, says that "childhood abilities—or lack thereof—are not a crystal ball of success. No age-related level of achievement is either a golden ticket or a locked gate."[7] In fact, many child prodigies do not develop into remarkable adults. They may become technically proficient in a particular discipline, such as writing or mathematics, but that does not translate necessarily into the skills needed for adult success. Shenk believes that many of these high-achieving children become "hobbled by the psychology of their own success" and grow averse to risk-taking.[8] Unfortunately, it is the very act of persisting, being willing to step out of one's comfort zone and tolerate frustration and failure, that contributes to adult success.

More and more evidence suggests intelligence and other talents are "malleable," influenced by not only one's environment but also the effort put into cultivating his skills or gifts. Studies such as Dweck's suggest that parents, as part of the environment, can and do affect their children's motivation. What parents have to contend with is that the influence they have over their children shrinks with time. Young adults do have their own lives, often very separate from those of their parents. As they grow older, the advice and suggestions parents have to offer will be weighed against those of other sources—friends, teachers, therapists, colleagues, religious leaders, and so on. Parents of teenagers often panic, hoping to instill all of their values in their children before they leave the nest. Alas, there is only so much of their legacy that will be carried on. Still, parents have an opportunity to enrich a child's experiences. Shenk's work, among other things, is a testament to the individual's capacity to grow and change both because and in spite of his genetic signature.

Culture also plays an important role in a child's development. Unfortunately, among many in the millennial generation, a starter job with minimal but honest pay is frowned upon. Expectations are high in young people seeking their first paycheck. They want a "cool" job that pays well and is not boring. This makes some sense given their unprecedented access to prominent writers, politicians, celebrities, and business leaders through social media channels such as Facebook and Twitter. However what is rarely published on such sites are reports of arduous work days, penny pinching, and the banal obligations that often come en route to distinguished careers. Becoming a writer for *The Daily Show* or a prominent fashion designer probably won't be the next step after a bachelor's degree. Often children complain that there are no good jobs when what they are really saying is that there are no good "dream" jobs.

For some children, having a car bought and paid for by their parents becomes a prerequisite for beginning the job search. "How do you expect me to find work if I don't have a car?" you may have heard your son or daughter say. Isn't this putting the cart before the horse? Those who are truly motivated to work will figure out a way to get there: maybe that means taking the city bus, finding rides from friends or family, or leasing a car with money from their first paycheck. In any case, they will do what it takes. Another common excuse for continued unemployment is rooted in classism. It is astonishing to me that at least 50 percent of my adolescent clients rule out fast food work or occupations in agriculture (picking fruits and vegetables on a farm) as employment options. They would rather sit at home and depend on their parents' income to support them, it seems, than do work they feel is beneath them.

Many of the same parents who complain that their children are unmotivated to work are the ones perpetuating these classist, and ultimately debilitating, attitudes. While working as a school psychologist, I was told by some parents that they did not want their young people working with any of the "three Fs": food, flowers, or filth—industries which they looked down on as menial and degrading. Of course there is certainly a point to be made that our children should follow their passions and pursue career paths that will lead to fulfillment. We don't want our children to enter a job where they will feel trapped and unvalued. But there is also a paralyzing effect that can come from waiting too long for the perfect opportunity. Being willing to do humble work, regardless of your ability or socioeconomic status, teaches lessons beyond the specific duties of the job. To name just a few: the importance of working effectively with others, the value of arriving and leaving on time, the necessity of going to work when you are tired or don't feel one hundred percent. Starter jobs teach work ethic. Unfortunately, the values some parents impart in their children lead not to an attitude of enterprise but to an attitude of entitlement.

Many Americans look at immigrants from impoverished countries with pity and condescension. They are poor or they lack opportunity. But in at least one area they are more fortunate than many native-born citizens — they are not held back by the cultural expectation life will be easy. The authors Thomas Stanley and William Danko examine America's wealthy extensively in the fascinating book *The Millionaire Next Door*. According to their research, at least 80 percent of American millionaires are "first-generation" rich who did not receive any inheritance, nor for that matter did they feel disadvantaged because of it. A sizeable number of the rich are first-generation Americans and entrepreneurs who themselves demonstrate "thrift, discipline, low consumption, risk, and very hard work."[9] They want their children to have a better life, and they pay substantial education costs to help them get there.

Economic deprivation combined with the belief in American opportunities created a spark in these individuals that led to their success. They overcame adversity and set goals that required delayed gratification. They worked assiduously and their hard work paid off—not immediately—but many years later.

According to Stanley and Danko, second generation immigrants typically do not follow in their parents' footsteps. With more education, they may attain the "better" lives their parents wanted for them. But with these lives comes the expectation of finer, more expensive material possessions and greater consumption. Within one to two generations, Danko and Stanley claim, they become Americanized and part of the "high consuming, employment-postponing generation." Reflecting on the life of one entrepreneurial immigrant named "Victor," the authors see a man who by thrift, hard work, and low consumption positioned himself to provide more for his children. His offspring, rather than following their father's lead and carrying on his business, became highly educated professionals. An unintended consequence of their class rise, however, was an increase in conspicuous consumption and a corresponding decline in wealth. Victor's grandchildren, it seems, may stray even further from the values of thrift and hard work. "This is why America needs a constant flow of immigrants," the authors write. "These immigrants and their immediate offspring are constantly needed to replace the Victors of America."[10]

Ever since the era of the Great Society under Lyndon Johnson, our government has attempted to tackle inequities and inequalities with federal programs. President Johnson oversaw the enactment of more than forty major new programs in a massive effort to improve standards of living and health, create jobs, increase educational achievement, and support the arts. Headstart, Job Corps, VISTA, Medicaid and Medicare, Food Stamps and higher education legislation are all examples. There is little doubt that such programs were devised with good intentions and have assisted many Americans. However even Lyndon Johnson, according to his top domestic aide, Joseph Califano,[11] had concerns that welfare programs without work incentives would have unintended consequences. He was right.

One such consequence was the dismantling of the family unit in inner cities. No program illustrates the problems of the welfare system more clearly than Aid to Families with Dependent Children (AFDC). When the program was first established in 1935, two-parent families were ineligible for assistance, even if the father was unemployed and the family was needy. In essence, women received money for not working, but only if the father was out of the picture. That law was amended in the 1960s, but there are still significant restrictions placed on welfare assistance for two-parent families. The 1996 welfare reform law, which included Temporary Assistance for Needy Families (TANF), has worked to end such constraints, but there is nevertheless a powerful disincentive for dual wage earning in the two-parent family: the income of the second adult may be counted against the family in determining eligibility and benefits.[12]

Entitlements did not create motivation, but led to its erosion. It was not until Congress enacted the 1996 legislation that there would be some limits placed on what many considered runaway spending. What we have learned is that without incentives to change behavior, money given away—whether to women on welfare or to children of the affluent—has negative consequences.

This does not mean that parents should create an impoverished environment in which to raise their adult children. But neither should they invest significant financial and emotional resources without expectations. Stanley and Danko use the term "outpatient economic care" to describe economic gifts and other seemingly charitable acts of kindness given to adult children and their grandchildren by parents. In one study, they compared the household net worth and annual household income of two groups of adult children of the same age: one who had received monetary gifts, and the second who had not. In eight of ten occupational categories, those children who had received gifts had less net worth than their counterparts. Stanley and Danko concluded that "the more dollars adult children receive, the fewer they accumulate, while those who are given fewer dollars accumulate more."[13] Moreover, they found that giving cash gifts to adult children "is the single most significant factor that explains lack of productivity among the adult children of the affluent."[14] In short, the adult children who were given money used it to consume goods, not to educate themselves or seek careers of their own.

Stanley and Danko's book, as interesting as it is, is only a narrow look at success defined in financial terms. Each of us has our own definition of what success looks like for our children and ourselves. A modest but well-respected career in the arts is a success for some, just as the job of a teacher, civil servant, therapist, machinist, electrician, or truck driver appeals to a different mind. The bottom line is that we want our children to be able to make their way in the world and be reasonably happy doing so.

Expecting to find millionaires to be a collectively materialistic group, Stanley and Danko were astonished by the results of their research. They found that millionaires are typically married, live below their means, drive older cars, wear inexpensive suits, and have lived in their homes more than twenty years. Two-thirds are self-employed in low-profile occupations: they are welders, contractors, rice farmers, accountants, and pest controllers. While the millionaires mastered the art of attaining wealth, they did not view money as their end goal. They recognized that many things have more significance than money—health, good relationships, integrity, and a loving family, to name a few.

So what can parents do to help their children, while conveying the values of hard work and motivation? One strategy is to take a look at what motivates adults to learn. Arguably the definitive volume in adult education, first published in 1973, is *The Adult Learner*, by Malcolm S. Knowles, with Elwood Holton and Richard Swanson. The authors posit several assumptions about adult learners that differentiate them from child learners:[15]

1. *Adults need to know why they need to learn something before they willingly try to learn it.* They will put much more effort into mastering something if they see its relevance to their lives.

2. *Adults deeply want to be recognized by others as capable of self-direction.* They resist and are hostile to instruction if they think others are imposing their wills on them.

3. *Adults bring their own experiences to a learning situation.* This can be an advantage or a disadvantage. Their prior experiences can add to a new learning situation, or may limit their openness to fresh ideas. Either way, their self-image will be tied to the experiences they have had.

4. *Adults' readiness to learn is tied in to their developmental stage and what tasks need mastering to move on.* Thus, the dependent young man's readiness to learn about saving and investing money will hinge on his being able to earn money in the first place.

5. *Adults want and need real-life application for whatever they are learning.*

6. *Adults are motivated by both external and internal factors, but internal pressures (e.g. more job satisfaction, self-esteem, quality of life) are more powerful.* Normal adults do move in the direction of wanting to grow and develop.

Here are some additional suggestions:

1. *It is clear that temperament and inherent traits have something to do with motivation.* You may alter your child's environment, but not everyone wants to be CEO or top of his class. Your first challenge is to recognize and accept who your adult child is. Your job is not to mold your child into the person you want him or her to be, but to assist your child in finding his or her own healthy path.

2. *If your child seems stalled in his or her ongoing development, work at understanding what is going on.* Invite him or her to talk about his or her future dreams, as well as what may be standing in the way of their achievement. Ask your child what he or she absolutely does not want to end up doing, i.e., what would be her nightmare future? In what kinds of settings does your child prefer to work (outside or in an office, business attire or casual)?

3. *Get outside input to help identify your child's strengths and interests.* Local community colleges offer vocational interest and aptitude testing that can be beneficial for people at all ages and in various stages of their career development.

4. *Once you have identified strengths, interests, and challenges, begin putting together a plan.* Have your son or daughter identify a long-term goal. It may be that your child wants to be in his or her own apartment within a year, or perhaps your child wants to pay off his or her car payments or start school.

5. *Work backwards to show your child how to arrive at his or her goals.* Drawing up this plan on paper is a good idea. Young adults need to be able to see the connection between their initial, small steps and more far-reaching goals. A Personal Planning Worksheet for Young Adults is found in appendix C. Use it as is or modify it to better suit your child's needs.

6. *Decide on how you will help your child along the way.* If your child has difficulty managing money, there are several approaches you can take. Some parents make their child sit down with them weekly to track expenditures and income. Others take over the child's checking account and, if necessary, have him or her write out a monthly budget while they monitor the account and provide guidance. In either case, it is a good idea to set reasonable thresholds for saving and spending.

7. *Be sure that you have clear expectations for your child.* That may be making consistent rent payments, following through with necessary medical appointments, or contributing to cooking dinner or cleaning the home. Praise your child's efforts and acknowledge your understanding of how difficult fulfilling these expectations may seem.

8. *Do not expect smooth sailing in this process.* Progress is not a simple series of steps that automatically lead to one's goals. You are the person who most cares about your adult child. Your son or daughter truly does not want to disappoint you. When you convey your faith in his or her ability to do the work needed, you send a powerful and reinforcing message.

9. *Do not let yourself become dissuaded by temper tantrums.* This is part of your child's resistance to growing up. Agree to resume your talks when he or she can speak respectfully to you.

10. *Remember, you are helping your child take critical steps in his or her development.* Your child is fortunate to have you on his or her side. However, if the difficulty you have working with your child exceeds

your ability to "hang in there," recognize your own needs and take appropriate action. You should not be working harder than your child.

11. ***Take some time to think about the outcome that you want for your child.*** Is it in line with the kind of outcome he or she is seeking? Be prepared to come to terms with differences between your dream for your child and his or her own dream. It can be very helpful to get input from others, including therapists and others who know your child.

CHAPTER SEVENTEEN

Parenting in the New Economy

The Trend toward Mutigenerational Living

The affluence of the 1990s and early twenty-first century is becoming a fading memory for far too many of us and our children. All of us are adjusting to a new economic reality. Not only do we feel it directly in our wallets and in the value of our homes, but we see friends, neighbors, and our own adult children losing jobs. For the first time in decades, Americans believe that their children may not have as good a life as they had. We see signs of the distressed economy in the bailouts of insurance companies, auto manufacturers, and the US banking system. We see it in the international debt crisis and the collapse of the Greek economy. And while it is true that these new economic realities affect us all, our children face arguably the greatest challenges due to their age. They are entering an increasingly competitive market-place, in which stronger international competition and smaller, more light-footed workforces have made their career choices and financial investment very different prospects than they were for members of our generation.

One of the results of this economic shift has been a rethinking of family living arrangements. For decades the multigenerational family was culturally unpopular. Now it is making a comeback. According to the Pew Research Center, the median age of first marriages has gone up by five years since 1970. The average male marries at twenty-eight and the typical woman at twenty-six.[1] With a longer time spent being single, many individuals in their twenties see the family home as a good place to be—either to save money before going to college or entering the workforce, or to return to between jobs. In 1980, just

11 percent of adults ages twenty-five to thirty-four lived with family. In 2008, the figure was 20 percent. Those young adults are frequently saddled with student loans, which can be difficult to pay back in a stuttering economy. High school and college graduates often cannot afford the cost of rent in areas where they'd like to live, and some cannot even find work. Another factor influencing the shift to multigenerational living, according to the Pew report, is the increase in immigrants from Latin America and Asia. For many of these new Americans, the family is the social security system. They are accustomed to multigenerational living because that is how they lived in their countries of origin.

The trend toward extended family households is seen across all demographics. Part of this has to do with the rise in single motherhood. When there is a young mother with no partner to help raise her children, the natural place to turn is her family. Statistics from a 2010 Pew report show that a record 41 percent of all births in this country were to unmarried women in 2008, compared to just 28 percent in 1990.[2] Looking at racial and ethnic differences, we find that 72 percent of the births to black women are to unmarried mothers, followed by Hispanics (53 percent), whites (29 percent), and Asians (17 percent). The highest rate of increase in births to single mothers has been among whites—69 percent in the past twenty years.

It is difficult to deny the challenges arising from the fact that single parents generally have less money than their married counterparts. Social welfare programs have stepped in to assist, but in many cases these programs only further have contributed to the decline of fathers consistently present in the households of their children. Without the support of a second adult, mothers look to their extended family for advice and assistance. Grandparents and other adults can share in the child care, serve as role models for the children, and bring additional financial stability to the family.

This last point, the financial benefit of multigenerational living, appears to be more important than ever. In recent years, the economy of several modern, industrialized nations has been in something of a tailspin. Greece's unemployment rate in the second quarter of 2011 stood at 16.3 percent, an historical high for that nation.[3] According to a report of the BBC,[4] heavy borrowing, accompanied by soaring public spending, a doubling in public wages, and widespread tax evasion have all contributed to the country's woes. Greece is currently undergoing stringent austerity measures required for bailout funding from the European Union. Ireland and Portugal have also been bailed out by the European Union (EU), and Italy is under pressure from the EU to reform its labor markets and judicial system.[5]

One result of these economic struggles is a shortage of jobs offering young people the living wages necessary to live independently. Throughout much of Europe and Asia, a new vocabulary has been created to describe the phenomenon of adult children living at home. The Prudential Corporation in England coined the word KIPPERS (Kids in Parents' Pockets Eroding Retirement Savings) to describe adults in their twenties and thirties who live with their parents.[6] Italy has its bamboccioni (Big Thumb-Sucking Babies); and the Japanese have "parasite singles," the term author Yamada Masahiro uses to describe the nation's young men and women who enjoy carefree lifestyles while living at home with their parents. According to Masahiro, 60 percent of Japanese single men and 80 percent of Japanese single women from the ages of twenty to thirty-four live at home.[7]

Many social critics believe the increase in children living at home is motivated not solely by the economy, but by a generational malaise. The Japanese psychiatrist Tamaki Saito points out in a recent article in the *Mainichi Daily News* that Germany has its "nesthockers," Austria its "Mama Hotels," and France its "Tanguy Syndrome," the last of these named for a film in which the main character refuses to move out of his parents' home.[8] The convergence of such reports among writers in even the most economically prosperous European countries attests to an eroding work ethic, an unwillingness among children of this generation to enter a professional career and make their own way.

Still, the role of the difficult economy cannot be ignored. Here is one scenario emerging in many US families: a young adult, sometimes but not always a college graduate, moves back home with his parents to stockpile his savings. Both the parents and the adult child know that the arrangement has a time limit, and the parents agree not to charge rent during that interval. Under this agreement, the young man is able to put away an additional $1,000 a month that would have gone to his landlord.

Here is another scenario: a young woman decides on a career change. Knowing this means an additional two years of schooling, she moves in with her mother, so that she can afford her classes and not accumulate additional student loans she will need to pay off after she graduates. Relatively unheard of a generation ago, the move back home is becoming increasingly common—and not just among the un- or underemployed. Confronting what some view as the increasingly likely prospect of a difficult and prolonged economic recovery, we can expect to see more of it in the coming years.

Planning for Multigenerational Living

In the current economic climate, your adult child's returning home is not necessarily a sign of laziness, incompetence, or poor money management. But if your adult child plans on moving in with you, it is time to do some serious planning. Consider your space, your resources, and your values and establish some clear expectations before moving day arrives. Most families keep things informal. If that works for you, fine. A more formal tenancy plan is also appropriate. Regardless of your preference, be sure to communicate the guidelines to your child before making new living arrangements.

A good first step is to clarify why your daughter is moving in. Is she moving back to pay off bills? Is she saving money for a first home or for graduate school? The answers to these questions will set the tone for the arrangement. You may or may not feel called upon to help your adult child structure her payment arrangements, but you should at least be aware of how money is being spent. Parents are often surprised that their children have very little financial awareness, especially when it comes to using debit and credit cards. Without sufficient insight as to the responsibilities accompanying their spending, children can amass large debts that make it virtually impossible for them to live on their own.

Before you even discuss money, ask yourself if it is a good idea to allow your child to live at home. Has she been evicted? Does she have any outstanding legal problems? A rude or malicious boyfriend? Depending on your own circumstances and the severity of your child's problems, you may not be in the best position to invite her into your home.

Have an honest discussion with your child. Insist that she is clear about her reasons for moving home, and ask yourself if you are ready for the changes her residency will mean for your family. Job loss is one of the more common reasons for adult children to return home and, if that is the case, you may have a very depressed young person arriving at your doorstep. While you may welcome the opportunity to help, your child may feel like she is taking a huge step backwards. Be aware of her fragile emotional state as you talk to her, and remind her that staying with you is not a permanent solution but an intermediary measure until she gets back on her feet.

Don't ignore your own motivations for inviting your child back home. Do you want to help her, or are you in need of help yourself? Under no circumstances should the living arrangements be the same as when your child was a teenager living in your care.

While your adult daughter may not know how long she is going to live with you, be sure to set a reasonable expectation as this reduces uncertainty. Circumstances change and six months might extend to twelve. One parent in the household may be more understanding of a longer stay than the other and compromise may be needed to ensure everyone is satisfied with the plan.

Another consideration is the schedule kept in the home. If you leave for work at 5:30 a.m. and go to bed at 9:30 p.m., will it disturb your sleep if your unemployed daughter rolls in at 3:00 a.m.? This is something to be addressed before you agree to a move-in arrangement. Perhaps your bedroom is far enough from hers that her late arrivals will not bother you, but know what you can live with. If your child has been on her own for a year or more, she undoubtedly will bristle at the idea of a curfew. Arranging for how your child can come and go without disturbing your sleep may be a better alternative than trying to maintain a curfew that will be consistently challenged.

What can be especially frustrating for a parent is to leave for work and see her unemployed son or daughter asleep in bed. In the parent's mind, the child looks as though he or she is not engaged in job-seeking at all, and sometimes that is true. Be absolutely clear as to your expectations. For children who seem motivationally challenged, you may want to require proof of the places they have contacted for jobs.

If there is a significant other in your child's life, be clear as to whether or not they will be staying over on a regular basis. Equally important is whether you are comfortable with the way the two treat one another. A number of parents express dismay at the stress brought into their lives by arguments between their child and her partner. Do you have room to give the couple privacy? Will you be able to distance yourself from the often turbulent circumstances that characterize relationships among young adults in their early twenties? In the case of extreme friction, are you prepared to ask your daughter's romantic partner to leave? Finally, are you ready for the possible backlash from your adult child, if you decide to regulate her partner's visits?

Even if your child is not living with someone, she probably will want the same freedoms she enjoyed in her own apartment—staying up late, listening to loud music, inviting overnight visitors. Consider your values and the physical layout of your home. If your daughter's bedroom is adjacent to yours, you may have objections. Remember, it is your house and you are entitled to feel comfortable there. Parents who think they are very open-minded might be surprised to learn their adult daughter *may be hoping* they set a boundary, if only to avoid embarrassing situations.

Does your adult child have children who are moving in as well? This can be a wonderful opportunity, a rare chance for three generations of a family to share in the pleasures of having a newborn to cuddle and care for. It can also be quite stressful. Is your daughter expecting you to be available for child care? Are you prepared for such responsibility? With three generations under one roof, there undoubtedly will be meaningful differences in parenting styles. When do you step in and when do you refrain from giving your suggestions and advice? Many of these questions will be answered for you as you tackle the demands of multigenerational living. But important considerations such as how to handle crying in the night, how to keep the child safe from injury, and how babysitting duties will be handled need to be discussed ahead of time.

Parents who have had their home to themselves for any period are accustomed to a level of privacy. This changes when an adult child moves in. Of course privacy is a two-way street. Your daughter will be most comfortable if she senses your respect for her boundaries. When the door to her room is shut, that is a signal she wishes not to be interrupted. Respect that signal. When your child is not home, do you stay out of her area? You ought to if you want her to respect your own boundaries. If she is unwilling to respect your privacy or you fear that she can't be trusted around your personal belongings, you may choose to put a lock on your bedroom door. This is also a wise step if you have good reason to be suspicious of your daughter's trustworthiness or that of her friends. In families where tensions run high due to the irresponsible behavior of an adult child, parents sometimes have the young adult leave the house when they leave, regulating the child's entry and exit from the home.

Whether you charge your child to live in your home will depend on your son or daughter's work status and ability to pay, as well as your own circumstances. Is there going to be an expectation of household chores or services in lieu of rent? Will you allow your son or daughter to stay with you rent free in order catch up on her bills? Know and agree on such matters in advance. One family I worked with allowed their daughter to move back into their home under the pretense of saving money. Happy to see their daughter finally getting her finances in order, they let her stay without charge. Two months into the arrangement, she bought a $15,000 car. Immediately, they rethought the arrangement. If you do plan to collect rent, make sure you understand your child's financial profile and have a due date and collection method in mind. This makes it easier to avoid confusion and long delays in payment.

One of parents' most frequent—and most defensible—gripes is that their adult children are procrastinators. This is an area where being assertive and direct as a parent can lead to real results. Here are examples of what I call "Procrastination Promises," each followed with an appropriate response:

> **SON:** "I don't know what happened to my unemployment check. When it comes, I'll give you some rent money."
>
> **PARENT:** "Let's call the unemployment office right now. I'll put the phone on speaker phone, so that we both can hear what they say and get to the bottom of it."
>
> **DAUGHTER:** "Yes, I'll sit down and make a budget as I promised, but I'm just too busy for the next two weeks."
>
> **PARENT:** Two weeks doesn't work for me. Let's look at our two schedules right now. I'm sure we can find the time in the next few days. I need the budget worked out before you use our car."

SON: "I'll get to that laundry that's on the floor, as soon as I get home from the movie. I don't have enough time to do it now. By the way, can I get some money for gas?"

PARENT: "You know, you're not keeping up your end of our agreement. I need to hold off giving you any more money until you're back on track with what you agreed to do here at home."

DAUGHTER: "I was going to go look for a job today, but I'm really tired. Besides, my friends tell me no one is hiring."

PARENT: "I'm glad you're in good health, so that a little fatigue won't keep you from searching. In fact, it will be energizing. This is an opportunity to show your friends that they just might be wrong."

SON: "Honestly, this is the last time I'm going to ask you for money. You don't want me driving around with no car insurance, do you?"

PARENT: "We're both on the same page on this one. Of course I wouldn't want that. So, I'm going to ask that you surrender the car keys until you've found the money to pay your portion of the insurance bill."

Drug or alcohol use can be a key factor prompting an adult child to return home. The child with a substance abuse problem generally has difficulties in other parts of his life. Be clear on the conditions that you need to have met in order for the child to live under your roof. That may mean not using at home, random or regular drug testing, or participation in a treatment program. Drug abusers are expert manipulators. Be prepared to check their stories against the facts, and have a plan in place if your child has become a risk to himself or others. Local shelters and housing programs are a good source of external support, if you have to insist that your child leave the home.

A drug or alcohol problem is not the only reason that eviction may be necessary. You are entitled to prohibitions against pornography, weapons, and other materials you do not wish to have in your household. If your son or daughter repeatedly ignores the agreed upon "rules," then it may be time for him or her to leave. The child who physically attacks you or someone else in the household is a safety threat, and the son or daughter who steals from the home or is verbally abusive is just as damaging on the psychological level. Any time a child knowingly threatens the health and safety of others or himself, or willfully violates the agreed upon rules in the household, it may be time for him or her to leave.

One of the risks of allowing an adult child with problematic behaviors to continue to live in the home is that the behaviors can become "normalized." The family continues to adjust and accommodate to keep the peace—or at least to prevent violence: "Oh, that's Danny. That's just the way he is." Be careful. If your child flies into a rage each time you are on the phone scheduling an appointment or talking to a friend, his behavior is not acceptable. One of the clues that the situation has become untenable is that other family members develop physical or emotional symptoms. Another sign of trouble is that your friends and acquaintances stay away from your house. Under no circumstances is it healthy to live in fear under your own roof.

Of course these are extreme cases, and many adult children are able to live under their parents' roofs for several weeks or months in relative peace and harmony. Saving money for a first home, seeking an affordable living situation between jobs, or returning to school and preparing for re-entry into an increasingly competitive workforce are valid reasons. Multigenerational living is indeed making a comeback. In the face of recent economic strain in the United States and abroad, increasing numbers of young graduates are returning home to prepare to live independently.

Returning home for a short time to brush up a resume, or save money for the future, may not be the worst choice a child can make, and seeing your twenty-five-year-old son or daughter show up at your doorstep with a suitcase shouldn't be cause for alarm. But you do need to handle the situation thoughtfully and set some basic expectations. Take the time to discuss the purpose of the arrangement and how it will work best for everyone. Whether you write out the plan or discuss it over lunch, consider that its success is subject to both you and your child following through. Above all, if your adult child is living in your home, remember that it is *your* home. Do not be hesitant to state your rules and preferences. Do not become a hostage to an unworkable situation. It *can* work, but it *will be* work. Careful planning, honest conversations with your child, and regular assessment are critical for the arrangement to be successful.

CHAPTER EIGHTEEN

The Bill of Rights for
Parents of Adult Children

From the original Bill of Rights to the ethical precepts put forth by PETA, Americans have historically, if imperfectly, embraced the notion that living creatures are entitled to certain rights. The curious thing about rights, however, is that their definitions are often adapted to the worldview of those proclaiming them. Pro-choice proponents speak of a woman's right to choose whether to terminate a pregnancy. Those against abortion proclaim the rights of the unborn. "Rights" sound virtuous, it seems, until one group's rights conflict with those of another.

Given the esteemed position rights occupy in the American tradition, it is surprising that so few have identified the rights of parents of adult children as a concern. Here I submit ten rights that I believe may contribute to the overall health and well-being of parents. For our purposes, a right shall be considered a legitimate and worthy condition to which one is entitled by virtue of being a parent.

1. *The Right to Be Free from Abuse*

Writers who focus on abuse tend to look at the obvious groups: children, dependent adults, helpless animals, and so forth. Parents, when introduced into the discussion, are almost universally assigned to the perpetrators' group. Some parents find themselves the victims of abuse by their children, and this can be physical as well as verbal or psychological (intimidation, rage, property damage). Non-physical offenses are just as serious and sometimes precursors to more direct acts of violence. In all cases, the abuser's goal is to gain or perpetuate control over another. Sadly, the pattern of mistreatment often goes unreported for many years because the parent is so accustomed to being bullied that she does not recognize the abuse for what it is. Worse, many cases of known abuse are kept secret. Parents are too ashamed to get therapeutic help and seek the healthy perspective that talking to others can provide. In families where abuse by children has been long existent, parents may even behave like battered spouses, believing they are somehow deserving of the pain meted out to them.

Abuse is never acceptable. If you find yourself in an abusive situation, set limits with your child. End abusive phone conversations, refuse to give time, money, or advice until you are treated appropriately, or don't meet with the child alone. If the situation escalates to the point that your safety is threatened, call the police or obtain a restraining order. Above all, exercise your right to stay free from abuse.

2. *The Right to Be Free from Guilt*

Parenting. Just hearing the word brings to mind a hefty responsibility. Parents feel accountable for what happens in their families, and when best intentions produce less-than-ideal results guilt creeps in. Guilt for the child's diet, for his school options, for the clothes on his back. Sometimes parents don't know what they have done to feel guilty. Nevertheless, their vulnerability to self-blame is a soft spot that adult children may use to take advantage. Some mothers and fathers may be subject to manipulation by an adult child who continues to hold them responsible for his delinquent behavior. Other parents find that their adult child has rewritten a seemingly normal family history. Only afterwards do such parents learn of their supposed crimes, often through a return to seemingly innocuous events in the past (e.g., "You *never* let me make my own decisions. I wanted to paint my room purple when I was fifteen and you wouldn't let me . . . Of course I overdrew my bank account, I never learned to control anything on my own.")

If you are an honest parent, you will own up to having made some mistakes along the way. At the same time, your child, if he is being fair, should not consider your missteps as the basis for each and every one of his character flaws. There are ways to atone for these mistakes, and a child who has empathy will honor your efforts to change. Don't be afraid to take corrective action. Talk to your adult child and ask for forgiveness, write a letter or email, get counseling with your child if he'll go with you.

No good purpose is served by being haunted with guilt forever. If your child will not forgive you, or you cannot forgive yourself, get help. Guilt that sinks into shame and self-loathing is unhealthy. It is far better to live life without the burden of guilt. It is your right.

3. *The Right to Peace of Mind*

Certain stages of life naturally come with turmoil. The transition from high school to college, one's first post-collegiate job, a break-up with a romantic partner, the birth of a child—all of these naturally involve stress as old ways of living make way for new ones. The same, of course, is true for parents whose children are reaching adulthood and leaving for college or the workforce. Becoming an empty nester requires an adjustment. For most people, the expectation is that, at some point, this will mean increased freedom and peace of mind. There may be new concerns, of course, such as the health and wellbeing of grandchildren, but, on the whole, life will be simpler.

For some families it is. They retire, downsize into a smaller home, take on new hobbies, and enjoy visiting their children and grandchildren. But other families find that their lives become increasingly strained when their children leave. There is no peace for a boomer parent whose adult child is struggling with issues such as substance abuse, spousal mistreatment, health or financial problems, or criminal activity. Add grandchildren to the picture, and the level of concern these families feel increases dramatically. When parents find that their child is in need of support, it is only natural for them to step in and help in whatever way they can. Still, it is important to set limits.

If you find yourself in one of these situations, you must "claim your peace." It will not just come to you, nor will it come as a one-time event. Claiming your peace means giving yourself permission to enjoy yourself at your job, have fun with friends, continue your hobbies, and take time to exercise. When you refuse to worry twenty-four hours a day, you are claiming peace. When you take a weekend getaway and surrender yourself to the pleasures of moment, you are claiming peace.

Not having your peace of mind is not only unhealthy; it also hurts your relationships and puts your professional life at risk. Does this seem impossible? If so, it is time to seek guidance from a caring friend or professional.

4. *The Right to Have Reasonable Expectations*

Expectations set the tone for how we view our relationships. If our expectations of others are too high, we will be chronically disappointed. Too low, and we risk others sinking to the disappointing bar that has been set. The question becomes, "What constitutes a reasonable expectation for an adult child?" Obviously, cultural variations, as well as variations within individual families, help determine the definition of "reasonable." Just the same, there are some basic behaviors which can and should be universally expected of young adults.

Young adults living at home should either be working or going to school, or both. They should contribute actively to the maintenance of the household, meaning, at minimum, picking up after themselves and their friends. If they are working, they should take care of as many of their own expenses as possible. Adult children employed full time should take sole responsibility for their personal expenses, including such budgetary concerns as their cell phone bill and car insurance payments. Depending on their income level, they should be asked to contribute to a share of the mortgage payment.

Illegal drug use or abuse of alcohol in the house is never acceptable. Respect your own philosophical and religious beliefs. If these prohibit the use of *any* controlled substances (e.g., tobacco, alcohol), then anyone who lives in your home should be held to those values. If you suspect drug or alcohol abuse, you have the right to require your son to get an evaluation. You may decide that the requirement for continued living in your home is his participation in a treatment program.

It is reasonable to expect that parents will be spoken to respectfully and that parents will return that respect. Parents' sleep schedules should be respected—meaning no late-night gatherings of a son's friends, if parents have to wake up early. Adult children may not want to abide by curfews. But if a son or daughter's late-night clubbing interferes too much with the parent's schedule, that may mean living at home is not an option for that child.

You may not want your adult child and his significant other sleeping together in your home. If that is your position, then it is reasonable to expect him to honor your beliefs. It is your home.

You have little to no control over an adult child's behavior when he is on his own. You can certainly expect him to be engaged productively in his career or education, but understand that he may not share that expectation.

5. *The Right to Be Imperfect*

It is more than merely your "right" to be imperfect. It is your reality as a parent and a person. Rather than aiming for perfection, do your thoughtful best, recognizing that perfection will never occur. You may learn that you are a better parent at some times in your life than others. You may find yourself with uncomfortable emotions such as jealousy for the achievements of your adult child. You may struggle with depression or substance abuse. All of these possibilities illustrate the futility of believing in one's own perfection.

If you're not a perfect parent, then what? Sometimes being a "good enough" parent is sufficient. A "good enough" parent recognizes her own strengths and limitations and, on balance, is comfortable that she is doing an adequate job. She acknowledges that there are advantages to being imperfect.

Others, including your own adult children, may have more empathy for you if you admit a degree of fallibility. You will enjoy yourself more because now you are not worried about having to be right all the time. You have the opportunity to model humility, the freedom to be authentic. Acknowledging your flaws also allows for learning. You open yourself to the beliefs of others, and your peers share more because they no longer feel like they're talking to supermom or superdad. You begin to exercise forgiveness.

6. *The Right to Decide What to Do with Your Own Money*

You are in charge of your money and where you choose to spend it. Give financially to your children if you so choose, but remember that doing so is a gift, not an obligation. In the affluent era in which baby boomers parented, many parents overindulged their children. Now, because of their tendency towards feeling guilty, some of these same parents cannot stop supporting their children financially. If you feel inwardly sick about a request for money, delay the request until you've had more time to think about it. Before making the decision, here are a few things to consider:

a. Adult children who don't work for what they get will not appreciate money in the same way as those who have worked for it. Parents do not owe their children the lifestyle to which they may have become accustomed. Nor do they owe their children money for traffic violations, fines, cars, furniture, frills, or even necessities. It is unwise to continue to give money to an adult child who uses it irresponsibly. If you do decide to give money, be clear as to whether the money is a gift or a loan. Do not use your gift as a weapon later to hold over your adult child's head.

b. If you have children who have moved back home, be crystal clear as to the financial expectations you have of them. Make a plan that encourages their eventual financial independence and works for both of you. For example, you might let your son stay rent-free in exchange for help around the house. You charge a small amount of rent, which you later return to him as a deposit on an apartment. Or, you help your daughter find community resources that set her on the path toward independent living once again.

c. Establishing boundaries with your money sends a powerful message to your children. You consider them the adults that they are. You have faith in them to handle their own finances. You allow them to experience delayed gratification, a sign of maturity. Don't expect gratitude if you constantly give money to your adult children with no expectation in return.

d. Respect your own financial limitations. You may wish you could contribute more, but are on a budget that prevents you from doing so. Don't bankrupt yourself: find other ways to be helpful. A wise therapist I know gave her granddaughters a huge box of fancy dress-up clothes she had purchased at thrift stores. This gift was far more meaningful and memorable than any expensive techno-treat they could have received.

7. *The Right to Decide What to Do with Your Time*

The most important gift you can give others or yourself is the gift of time. Distribute that gift with care. Your time is valuable. Like any precious commodity, if you give it away too freely, it will lose some of its value. Let's say you are always available to babysit your grandchildren, dog-sit your child's hound, or drive your friend to her doctor's appointments. You may be creating an expectation you will not be able to maintain—or worse, one that will be upheld to your detriment. Human nature is such that people who give too much of their time to others are often taken for granted.

Baby boomer women, as a rule, are accustomed to taking on multiple roles and juggling schedules to meet others' needs. Consequently, they are prone to having considerable demands placed on their time. In addition, many boomers find themselves sandwiched. How do they simultaneously meet the needs of their adult children and those of their aging, increasingly dependent parents?

Regardless of the demands placed on you, the important point is that you are in charge of your free time. Whether working in or outside the home, full or part time, you do not need an excuse to spend time doing nothing but relaxing. In fact, the busier your schedule, the more important it is to find some "down time."

Making a decision to be more protective of your time may conflict with the views of important people in your life. You may find that you don't want to babysit as often as you had anticipated, or that you have more in common with one family member than another. You may choose to shorten conversations that involve gossip and hearsay, or to engage in a new hobby that limits your availability at a moment's notice. Whatever choice you make, remember that your task is to make your own best decisions about how you spend your time. It is your right and your life.

8. *The Right to Say "No"*

It is no accident that "no" is one of the first words children learn. When young children make the connection between that single syllable and its impact on others, new worlds open. The word is screamed and shouted with delight as children realize they have the power of refusal. The right to say "no" may be the most crucial of all, as it is a prerequisite for all others. We must be able to say "no" to stop or prevent abuse, to claim our peace, to control our finances, and to manage our time.

Saying "no" is also good for our loved ones. Young adults are better prepared for real-life obstacles if they have heard "no" prior to moving

out on their own. Overindulged adult children who have never heard
"no" may have an especially hard time coping with rejection from a
hoped-for first job or promotion. "No" forces children to use their
imagination and forces adults to cope with delayed gratification.
Being unable to afford that new sofa for your daughter's den is not a
sign of your inadequacy. If you agree to buy the sofa when prudence
warrants saying "no," both of you lose. She gets the sofa, but also your
resentment. You feel unappreciated and act more guarded around her,
setting up a dangerous cycle.

Saying "no" makes a heartfelt "yes" more likely. The woman who
exercises her right to say "no" establishes boundaries with others that
allow her to enjoy her chances to say "yes." She will welcome the
opportunity to do for her adult child, friend, or spouse, what it is she
truly wants to do.

Engaging in your right to say "no" may displease your children,
friends, and colleagues. That does not mean you are doing something wrong; in fact, it usually means the opposite. You have chosen
to be authentic, rather than compliant; real rather than superficially
agreeable.

9. *The Right of Selective Association*

It is each parent's right to decide with whom she will associate. The
majority of adult children recognize this and do not interfere with
their parent's choice of friends, business associates, and romantic
partners. However, while the right may seem obvious enough as an
extension of one's personal freedom, it is a right that is not always
honored.

Three areas stand out as especially prone to conflict.

The first has to do with parental decisions regarding new partners.
Parents have the right to choose their partner or spouse, and adult
children should be tolerant of this choice. No matter how carefully a
parent exercises this right, her decision will touch her child at a deep
level. For example, a son may bristle at the idea of his mother's
becoming intimately involved with a new partner after the death of
her husband. Regardless of the quality of this new relationship, the
son may feel as though its existence infringes on the longstanding
emotional bond between his mother and father.

A second source of conflict has to do with the emergence of a new extended family. Adult children will not necessarily welcome another entirely new set of family members, nor the new holiday traditions accompanying them. Parents should be aware of the extent to which their choices stir their children's emotions. Discomfort with a new partner may have less to do with the parent's choice than the child's fear of losing his parent's attention. While an adult child's reaction should not dictate a parent's choice, the wise parent knows that his or her actions may elicit strong reactions that require attention. Talking to children about these concerns is essential to maintaining the stability of the relationship.

Finally, siblings may complicate the picture. Some adult children save their harshest judgment for their brothers or sisters. A compliant son may resent the help his parents offer his rebellious sister. One sibling may be ready to "write off" another whose lifestyle or habits conflict with those of the rest of the family. Adult children often are incapable of understanding a parent's unwillingness or inability to "give up on" a sibling, especially if that sibling has been abusive. While the adult child may have every reason to be concerned, it is still the parent's right to choose to have contact with each of her children. Only that parent can decide when, if ever, to sever a relationship with his or her child.

10. *The Right to Retirement*

The right to retirement is viewed as a given to most people. But traditional notions of retirement do not exist for everyone. Some adult children are incapable of living independently due to learning problems or other disabilities. Parents of these children face special challenges in planning for their children's futures. They must take into account their own needs, as well as their children's, when planning for later life expenses and living arrangements.

Unexpected tragedy, such as the untimely death of an adult child, does occur, and may result in grandparents becoming the primary caregivers of their grandchildren. However most of the time when the retirement "right" is given up, it is not due to a single event, but rather a series of decisions and events that result in parents having to continue working longer than originally intended.

Some parents who are compelled to defer plans for their retirement have adult children who've been struggling financially or emotionally for years. The parental motivation is well-intended: they love their children. But decisions to assist or not assist are complicated. If there are grandchildren involved, they often feel obliged to help. A grandparent's concern for the well-being of her grandchild, particularly if the child's parent is behaving irresponsibly, can be gut-wrenching. If at age sixty, a parent still feels responsible for his or her adult child's situation, giving assistance may seem like the only option.

Although every parent has the right to decide whether or not to cut a child off financially, it is useful to keep some things in mind. First, parents have a "right" to reap the benefits of a lifetime of work. There are times when financial assistance is appropriate, but no child is automatically owed a bailout. Second, there is no reason to believe that an adult child lacking a work ethic will suddenly change with "just one more small loan" from his mother or father (especially if there is addictive behavior going on). Simply insisting on responsibility on the part of your child will be ineffective unless you accompany that directive with action that enforces your message. Adult children have years in which to prepare for their own retirement. Don't be too quick to give away your own.

CHAPTER NINETEEN

Twelve Truths for
Parents of Adult Children

In the course of preparing this book, a number of "truths" emerged. I chose to list and expand upon twelve of them. They offer a summary of my conclusions based upon my research and interviews. I've presented them here for your consideration, and, hopefully, discussion with other parents of adult children.

1. *Love does not conquer all.*

We'd like to live by the simple sayings we heard growing up. "Love conquers all" is one of them. Parents who have struggled with difficult adult children know the injunction all too well. Many have told me that well-intentioned family members and professionals counsel them, quite simply, to love their child—as if the thought has never occurred to them. Too frequently, such advice-givers have no clue as to what the parent has gone through in the process of loving his or her son or daughter.

Another version of this theme involves a change in location. "Send her to live with us," relatives say. "We'll straighten her out." The change of scene and family members may yield results, but often, young people with deep-seated emotional issues simply take these problems from one household to another. Commonly, by the time an adult child has burned the bridge with her parents, she has developed a pattern of poor choices—substance abuse, anger problems, criminal convictions, etc.—which accompanies her to the new home.

The mantra that a mother should "just love her child more" ignores the uncomfortable reality that some children have profound psychological issues that prevent them from acknowledging or accepting love. If loving your child is tearing you apart or destroying your relationships with others, then your notion of loving needs careful re-examination. One-sided love, love that is rejected, discarded, or thrown back into a parent's face is not healthy. A more helpful form of loving may be to back off from helping or enabling your child, while allowing her to experience the consequences of her behavior. This gives her an opportunity to change and preserves your resources, be they emotional, physical, or material.

2. *Doing more and more for others will not bring love and respect.*

It is wonderful to give of yourself, but keep in mind your expectations and motives. Realistically, giving is not one hundred percent charitable. Often we give of ourselves to seek another's appreciation, attention, love, or respect, or to feel better about ourselves. For many of us, it feels better to be the giver, not the receiver, in a relationship. It seems like the morally "right" thing to do.

I urge you to be careful. Endless giving for others is counterproductive. A number of excellent books have been written about women who do too much and love too much.[1] They attest to the hazards of unrequited affection—dangers easy to understand in terms of romantic relationships or relationships among same-age friends, but more difficult to comprehend when we talk about giving in the context of our children. This latter kind of giving taps into our learned concept of what constitutes a good mother or a good father. In a very real sense, a mother is one who "gives" her children life. But healthy giving includes balance. When giving is healthy, a feeling of goodwill and appreciation is present in both the parent and the child. Neither party feels injured.

In the Depression era, most parents could not offer much for their children materially. Their own resources were few and constituted a natural boundary. But in the 1960s and 70s increased opportunity and wealth enabled parents to indulge their children. In many cases, there were no limits: the more parents did, the more that was expected of them. The consequence of their support, which often emerged in the form of emergency lifelines and cash infusions, was spoiled adult children: children who felt entitled and who, sadly, were incapable of meeting their own needs.

Parents and children who arrive in such situations are locked in an unhealthy cycle. What is intended as temporary help becomes expected. Parents feel exploited when they see inadequate effort on the part of their adult children, who come to rely too heavily on their support. Children resent their parents if the "help" is diminished or discontinued, whether that help is financial assistance, time, or other acts of generosity.

You are not an unloving parent if you reconsider your style of giving, particularly if it is not yielding the hoped for result: a more independent and functional adult.

3. *Loving and liking your adult child are not the same thing.*

I often tell parents attending my workshops that unconditional love is more easily practiced by grandparents than parents. Grandparents can laugh off some of the behaviors that make parents of young children frustrated, furious, and embarrassed. Having successfully endured years of challenges, they have a more relaxed perspective. Most grandparents do not feel the pressure and responsibility of the primary parenting role.

Our egos as parents are more directly entwined in the actions of our children. We love our children, but, at times, do not love their behavior. For the most part, our love withstands the challenging times because the deep bonds we have with our kids override the difficulties. We are fortunate if they grow into adults who are easy to love and to like. We feel in a state of grace because we have a child whom we respect and who has become a friend. But not all parents have that kind of connection. For many reasons, a parent may still love his child but not particularly like him. It could be the result of a personality clash, or disappointing behaviors that have eroded the relationship.

Parents who have been challenged with extreme behaviors by their adult children will likely have difficulty expressing unconditional love. They often feel two conflicting beliefs simultaneously: the desire to love a child whom they nurtured and guided, and disillusionment or heartbreak with that same child due to his actions. Their animosity is usually rooted in years of frustration, anger, hurt, and unmet expectations. Do not rush to judge the parent who admits to disliking his or her child. Most parents want nothing more than to love their children unconditionally. For some parents, however, years of disrespect and ingratitude have left them incapable of exhibiting this selfless and often painful kind of love.

4. *It is neither possible nor prudent to treat all your children equally at all times.*

Equal treatment of our children is impossible. We know this in our hearts, yet walk on eggshells to be impartial. From a young age, siblings sense real or imagined differences in how their parents treat them. "Marlene got the bigger piece of pie. Why do you always give her what she wants?" "Marlene just got a new car. Why should I drive Grandma's piece of junk?" This line of argument is manipulation. Don't fall for it.

At various times, one child may be more "deserving" of certain privileges and responsibilities than another. Should the adult daughter who wrecked her first two cars get the same financial assistance toward that next Mini Cooper as the son who drove his first car throughout college without incident? These kinds of questions get even more complicated when a family's employment and living situation change. Are the parents who lost one income due to an unexpected lay-off obliged to send their third daughter to a private school as they'd done for their first two children?

Parents learn about parenting as they raise their families. The wisdom gained from overindulging a first-born will come to bear in parenting subsequent children. All the same, a father's newfound wisdom may not be appreciated by his second child who is thereafter asked to mow the lawn and clean out the gutters in exchange for assistance with his car insurance payments.

From time to time, all parents inevitably have biases. The wise parent knows this and is attuned to whether these biases are reasonable or color her treatment of her children unfairly. When unsure of your motives, seek input from others. Think about what they have to say before making a judgment call. If your children ask why you are being preferential in your treatment, be honest. Perfectly equal treatment is impossible for two different people with their own interests, needs, and track records. Additionally, the timing of a request may make it impossible to honor. Your perspective, expectations, or circumstances may have changed.

5. *Guilt-making does not improve relationships.*

Many baby boomers confess to growing up in households in which guilt was used as a form of leverage or punishment. They were compliant with their parents' wishes because disobedience meant submitting to a burden of guilt. While the ability to experience guilt is part of one's moral development, inducing guilt should be done with care.

Endeavoring to make someone feel guilty as a way of influencing their behavior may foster compliance, but it comes with obvious disadvantages. Did it work for you when your mother shamed you into doing something you had no desire to do? Did it work for your mother? She may have elicited the behavior she wanted, but at what cost? Perhaps you did such a good job concealing your resentment that she never knew. More likely, your resentment was recognized by your mother as an "attitude" on your part; a desire to withdraw from her.

Feeling constant guilt is one of the primary reasons that people choose to withdraw from their loved ones. Anytime you have to quietly disgrace someone into taking the action you want, you win the battle but lose the war. It is far better to have an honest conversation about your needs, desires, and disappointments than to disguise your wishes through innuendo. What does it say about your relationship with your child if the only way you can obtain her cooperation is to compel her to feel bad about herself?

The capacity to levy guilt, as we saw in chapter five, is necessary to guarantee moral behavior in a civil society. Still, when used as a weapon to maintain contact with our children or to control them, guilt is not productive.

6. *Adult children need to feel "heard" before they will listen.*

This truth should come as no surprise. We all feel a need to have our ideas and beliefs recognized and acknowledged by others. Not feeling understood or "heard" is a major theme underlying many conflicts that bring couples and families to therapy. A wife may think that her husband does not "get" her, while a husband may think that his wife is deaf to his concerns. Both find it impossible to heed the suggestions or advice of the other without irritation or resentment. The same applies to the relationships we have with our children. An adult daughter may view her mother as bossy and unyielding, while the mother thinks her daughter doesn't respect what she has to say. Neither feels heard nor understood by the other, and they become stuck.

The lesson is that advice, however wise, will not be heard *unless and until* the recipient feels understood. The missing step is the acknowledgment of the other's feelings. The mother who wants to improve her relationship with her daughter has a better chance of doing so if she can listen to her daughter's feelings in earnest and acknowledge their validity. Realize that acknowledging feelings does not necessarily mean agreeing with them. But the very act of recognizing someone's position, even as it differs from your own, is a powerful facilitator for communication. The listener will begin to lower his "wall" of defenses and become more open to suggestion.

7. *Sometimes the loving thing to do is to let your child experience unpleasant consequences.*

In parenting, there is a time for nurturing and a time for stepping aside, a time for protecting and a time for letting consequences happen as they may. Allowing a child to experience hardship runs counter to our instinct to nurture and protect our children. What kind of mother does not help her child? But sometimes helping involves stepping aside and letting our children learn what it means to struggle, even if this means short-term disappointment or failure.

Hopefully, as we mature as parents, we learn when to move in to protect our children, and when to back off. The mother who tires of running her child's lunch to school because he constantly forgets it helps her child be more conscientious by letting him experience a day without his lunch. The nurturing stance she took in the past did not improve his behavior, and he likely will not miss many more lunches before he begins remembering—or learns how to creatively broker food from his friends.

Experiencing the natural consequences of their actions prepares young adults for independent living. The young woman who has to pay her rent in early adulthood is going to be better off, ultimately, than the one who never has to face the unpleasant consequence of paying late or not paying at all. As painful as it can be to let our children experience hardship and failure, they will fare better if we allow them to confront these natural consequences on their own.

8. *You cannot choose your child's partner.*

Your child will choose a partner based upon his particular tastes and preferences. The reasons why your child's partner has a navel ring and twelve cats may be a mystery that you never solve. But it is not your business to do so. Your challenge is to respect his choice, even if you feel like screaming that he should run the other way. For the sake of your relationship with your child, find the positive qualities in that person. You can assume that if forced to choose between you and his partner, your child will go with his partner. Don't make that an easy choice for him. You may have years of life experience that he lacks, but no adult son wants his mother to sound the alarm when he is in love.

Letting events follow their natural course allows your adult child to learn and grow. If you intervene in your son's relationship by unsolicited advice-giving, he may get caught up in the defense of his partner and be unable to see the situation clearly. Take the high road. If you need to react to an adversarial partner or spouse, make sure you focus on the objectionable behaviors, not on the person's character. In the event their relationship ends—assuming you have not been unduly critical of your adult child or his spouse along the way—you will be in a better position to maintain a relationship with your child. Additionally, if the relationship is rekindled, you will not have created a legacy of ill will to overcome.

It is another matter if you think the relationship is abusive. Then being direct with your adult child about your observations and concerns is warranted. Besides offering your support—in whatever

form it takes—you can give him information about community resources. If your child is the object of the abuse, you may notice that
his partner tries to isolate him from his family and friends. In fact,
such efforts are often a clue that something is amiss. In healthy, se-
cure relationships (as long as the parents themselves are mentally
healthy), the family is typically welcomed into the lives of the couple.

And finally, never condone your child's spouse or partner abusing
you. Not only are you protecting yourself by taking appropriate action
(e.g., confronting the behavior, withdrawing contact if necessary), you
are modeling healthy behavior for your adult child. Even if grandchildren are involved, your very first commitment must be to maintaining your safety and well-being.

9. *Only you can decide how long to "hang in there."*

All emotionally healthy people have limits and boundaries; however,
there is no simple algorithm to define one's breaking point. Many
well-meaning parenting experts have discouraged already frustrated
parents by offering pat advice: "Never give up on your children." Be
careful of such wisdom. It is dangerous to ignore an adult child's irresponsible behavior, or to think that the solution to his problem must
be within your grasp, if only you do or say the right thing.

Therapists' waiting rooms are full of parents who are convinced
they are accountable for all of their child's problems. They are accused of enabling or abandoning their children. One such parent,
who was caught up in years of rescue attempts which were system-
atically resisted by her son, asked me what I would do in a similar situation. Having observed her anguish over a period of many
months, I replied that I couldn't say for certain that I would have
done anything differently. "It is not my place," I added, "to tell you
how long to hang in there with your son." However, I also gave her
some practical advice. On the basis of what she'd told me, it appeared that her son was unwilling or unable to make use of her assistance. I told her it was okay to shift her efforts from trying to
heal him toward working on healing herself.

Therapists, family, and friends can make suggestions, but only you can decide when you are ready to stop "hanging in there" for your child. At first there will likely be some ambivalence about the decision, but there is a time to stop directing all of your resources to a difficult adult child. Redirect your energies to those who can appreciate and value you and what you offer.

10. *Disagreement may be a sign of emotional growth.*

More than one mother has said to me, "I am happy when everyone else is happy." Mothers like confluence; we are content when everyone is getting along. Yet, understanding the phenomenon of separation and individuation means recognizing the importance of young adults being able to have views in opposition to those of their parents. We should expect disagreement and recognize it as a sign of emotional growth. Let's say a mother tells her adult daughter about the clothes she plans to take on a trip, and her daughter criticizes her choices. The mother can bemoan her daughter's reaction, feeling hurt by what she perceives as criticism, or frame this exchange as her daughter expressing an autonomous, if rudely put, view.

What is important here is not so much the content of the daughter's message, but the legitimacy of her having a different opinion than her mother. The mother's clothing choice is simply the inciting event for differentiation. When the mother recognizes it is healthy for her daughter to have her own opinions, she sends two important messages: first, agreement is not a requirement for being loved; and second, she will be okay if her daughter stands on her own.

Almost without exception, each generation claims their ideas are superior to those of their predecessors. Despite the imperfections in our culture, we would not have achieved nearly the progress we have if successive generations feared the differentiation process.

11. *What is normal for one family is abnormal for another.*

There are as many kinds of families as there are varieties of wines. Children in a nuclear family believe their lifestyle is normal. But ask another child whose grandparents live in the same home as his parents and he, too, will tell you that his family is normal. Be wary of comparing your family to those of others. Blended families, extended families, single-parent households, grandparent-led families, and families with gay or lesbian parents exist alongside the traditional nuclear family and are just as capable of raising healthy adult children.

The means by which people come together, solve disputes, love, worship, and grieve vary profoundly from one family to the next. Normal in one family might mean spirited debates with shouting and head shaking, while soft voices and suppressed feelings may prevail in the house next door.

Two sisters who grew up within the same household can follow completely different trajectories. One may embrace the arts, while the other becomes a star athlete. One may be laissez-faire about her appointments and personal finances, while the other micromanages every aspect of her life. These variations are natural and expected. The more important consideration is how the family is working for its members. Sometimes a parent and child have incompatible interests— the artistic child, for instance, who grows up in a family with a passion for fitness and athletics. Attuned parents will try to meet the needs of each child, even when those needs and preferences differ from their own.

12. *Sometimes the route to increased closeness lies in tolerating separateness.*

Often the very thing parents dread becomes a method for getting what they want. We fear the separateness that the process of differentiation brings. But it is not just the task of children to emancipate. Parents must allow and encourage that process. Some parents focus so little on themselves that their own individuation either never occurs or ceases to define their existence. When their children were young, parenting defined their identity and life revolved around that role. Now the time has come for a daughter to go off to college or marry, and there is a confusing wave of anxiety and depression. "I should be so happy for her right now. Why do I feel so much grief?"

We have to let go of our children for them to return to us. If they have sufficiently developed and matured, then upon "return" they will look and feel different. Even if a parent is fully understanding and prepared for the process, living through it is another matter.

Increased irritability with a parent is an indication that a young adult has not completely made this transition.

While there is no guarantee the outcome will be what we want, be assured that for true emancipation to occur, your child will have to experience at least an emotional, if not a physical, separateness from you. When this happens, she can better appreciate you for the person who you are. When she sees that both you and she are fulfilled as separate people, she will likely seek a deeper, more adult connection with you. And this is as it should be.

Acknowledgments

The idea for this book came out of my search, begun almost seven years ago, to find out how my fellow baby boomers were parenting their adult children. As a therapist, I'd looked for resources for my clients, only to find them mostly lacking. So, via word of mouth, I began to gather names, and then stories of how people were parenting. What I found was no perfect family, but dozens of very real families, and parents willing to share some of their most poignant moments with me. Thus, I must first thank them, the men and women who opened their lives, so that others could see the parenting journey for what it really is—sometimes gratifying and at other times quite difficult. Some of them met with me multiple times over several years, and were willing to give me updates via e-mail and evening phone calls.

Next, I want to thank Jeff Link, my editor at NTI Upstream, who guided me through the process of putting together a book that is professional, yet retains a conversational tone with my readers. He "got" my voice, and showed this first-time author the ropes, in taking a book to completion. Thanks also to Kimberley Cameron, my agent, who helped me fine tune my proposal so that it would be ready for a publisher. Because of her enthusiasm, we connected with NTI, who picked up my project at a time when new authors have difficulty getting into print.

If there is something I've learned along the way, it's the value of persistence and patience, taught to me by Nancy Bartley, in whose writing group I've participated for over four years. With her expertise and support, what began as an outline for a book became a proposal.

Nancy read and re-read my words innumerable times. And I read and re-read them aloud at our monthly writing group sessions. There is no way this book would have evolved without feedback from my fellow writers: Sheila Ball, Joan Brekke, Maggie Ellis, Barbara Harris, Evelyn Huff, Luci Baker Johnson, Nadine Joy, Liz Kranz , Yvonne Lutz, and Rea Scovill.

Many thanks to those authors who lend moral support to new writers, including Meg Waite Clayton, Louise Penny, and Louise Hendricksen. A "thank you" also goes out to Beth Laberto, of the Youngstown City Schools, who tracked down my mother's high school transcript from 1933.

I have only gratitude and respect for my clients who offered me encouragement along the way, and for my friends, who likewise showed their interest in what I'm doing.

And finally, I am blessed to have the steadfast and loving support of my family, especially my husband Robert and sons, Marcus and Jim, who have had unwavering faith in me. Without them, this book would never have been written.

- - - - - - - - - - - - -

Finding Your Parenting Style

One way to look at parenting is as a progression of "the three Cs." Parents move from being *choreographers* of their children's lives to *coaches* and, ultimately, to *consultants*. Within that progression parents tend to settle on a general approach, depending on their preferences and the preferences of their children. Conflict may arise when a parent wants one level of contact and their child prefers another. In these situations, it is important to recognize the dynamics that are in play. This appendix explores "the three Cs" and provides exercises for determining your preferences and those of your adult children.

1. *Parents as Choreographers*

In the early months and years of a child's life, parents should be playing the role of choreographers. The word choreography, derived from Greek (literally "dance-writing"), refers to the structures in which movement occurs. Mothers and fathers, while allowing for natural and spontaneous development, must choreograph their children's routines, as much as possible, to give their children boundaries and direction. That means planning for consistent meal times, nap times, play times, and bedtimes, as well as deciding which activities the youngster will participate in. A toddler cannot do this for himself. As the choreographer, the parent must establish structure for the child.

2. *Parents as Coaches*

Coaching is still very hands-on, but significantly less so than choreography. The coach is the director of operations of a team; he trains the players before the game, but once the whistle blows, events happen through the independent decision making of the players on the court.

In the realm of parenting, the coach is the parent who works from the sidelines. She watches her child at home, at play, in social situations, or at school. She is there with suggestions, but not in charge of every step the child takes. Best suited for the parents of school-age children and adolescents, the coaching role may take a variety of forms. Parents may coach their children in rules of social engagement and rules of etiquette, in caring for pets and respecting adults, and in understanding how to be gracious winners and losers. Because they have mastered many of these skills themselves, parents are able to pass on their accumulated wisdom to their children.

3. *Parents as Consultants*

A consultant, as most of us know, is a person referred to for expert or professional advice. Consultants give their opinions and recommendations, but they generally do not take it personally if their ideas are not followed. The consultant's advice is there to take or leave. As children grow into adulthood, parents often function in this capacity, offering their knowledge and assistance sparingly in matters such as home buying, childcare, and marriage and divorce counseling.

Below is a two-part exercise that allows you to reflect on the kind of contact you and your adult child have with each other. Read the statements and circle the responses that best describe your relationship. If you have more than one child, you may want to complete a separate survey for each. It is very possible that their differing styles, personalities, and needs will be reflected in your responses, as will your own needs.

PART ONE

ADULT CHILD EXPLORATION SHEET

1. My adult child uses me as a sounding board.
    never   sometimes   frequently   always

2. My adult child talks with me before making decisions.
    never   sometimes   frequently   always

3. My adult child asks for my input and advice, and follows my suggestions.
    never   sometimes   frequently   always

4. My adult child asks for my input and advice, but gets angry when I give it.
    never   sometimes   frequently   always

5. My adult child seeks my guidance in managing activities of daily living.
    never   sometimes   frequently   always

6. My adult child seeks my guidance in relationships.
    never   sometimes   frequently   always

7. My adult child seeks my guidance in career or educational matters.
    never   sometimes   frequently   always

8. I offer advice to my adult child without first being asked.
    never   sometimes   frequently   always

9. I have difficulty backing off, if I disagree with my adult child's decisions about relationships.
    never   sometimes   frequently   always

10. I have difficulty backing off, if I disagree with my adult child's decisions about his job or career.
    never   sometimes   frequently   always

11. I have difficulty backing off, if I disagree with my adult child's decisions about everyday matters.
    never   sometimes   frequently   always

12. My adult child shares too many of his problems with me.
    never   sometimes   frequently   always

13. I have confidence that my adult child can manage his own life.
    never   sometimes   frequently   always

14. My adult child confides in me.
    never   sometimes   frequently   always

15. My adult child would make better choices if he talked to me beforehand.
    never   sometimes   frequently   always

16. I wish my adult child would seek my input more frequently.
    never   sometimes   frequently   always

17. I wish my adult child would seek my input less frequently.
    never   sometimes   frequently   always

18. When I think about my role in my adult child's life, I feel like a
    choreographer   coach   consultant

LINDA M. HERMAN © 2013

As you read your responses, consider the kind of contact you have with your child and the kind you'd prefer. Are you more or, perhaps, less involved in your child's life than you would like to be? If you are acting as more of a consultant, you may realize you prefer the coaching role. Or just the opposite may be true. You might realize you want to be in a consulting role, while your son or daughter expects coaching about decisions large and minute. Make sure you are acting in the role best suited to your child's maturity level and your own preferences as a parent.

Don't worry if your preferences don't accord with your actual behavior; there is ample opportunity to fine-tune your parenting style and the level of contact you have with your child. If you're uncertain as to your adult child's expectations (when she comes to you nearly every day ready to unload her grievances), you might say something like, "I'm not sure if you want some advice from me, some suggestions, or if you just want me to listen." Pay attention to her response.

She'll most likely let you know. Even if your daughter is not clear, at first, as to what she wants from you, she may find comfort talking to you. Some children are reluctant to come right out and ask for help. Don't be afraid to be proactive in communicating with them.

Another way to explore your relationship with your child is to look more directly at your *own* needs and behaviors and the role your adult child takes in *your* life. Sometimes circumstances (or preferences) result in a role reversal, where the adult child is the advisor to the parent. Particularly when a parent ages or encounters major life or health problems, this may be the case. Consider the following statements and, once again, circle the responses that best fit you and your situation.

PART TWO
PARENTING STYLE EXPLORATION SHEET

1. I use my adult child as a sounding board.
   never   sometimes   frequently   always

2. I talk with my adult child before making decisions.
   never   sometimes   frequently   always

3. I ask my adult child for input and advice, and follow his or her suggestions.
   never   sometimes   frequently   always

4. I ask my adult child for input, but get angry when he or she gives it.
   never   sometimes   frequently   always

5. I seek my adult child's guidance in managing activities of daily living.
   never   sometimes   frequently   always

6. I seek my adult child's guidance in relationships.
   never   sometimes   frequently   always

7. I seek my adult child's guidance in career or educational matters.
   never   sometimes   frequently   always

8. My adult child offers me advice without first being asked.
   never   sometimes   frequently   always

9. My adult child has difficulty backing off, if he or she disagrees with my decisions about relationships.
   never   sometimes   frequently   always

10. My adult child has difficulty backing off, if he or she disagrees with my decisions about my job or career.
    never   sometimes   frequently   always

11. My adult child has difficulty backing off, if she disagrees with my decisions about everyday matters.
    never   sometimes   frequently   always

12. I share too many of my problems with my adult child.
    never   sometimes   frequently   always

13. My adult child has confidence that I can manage my own life.
    never   sometimes   frequently   always

14. I confide in my adult child.
    never   sometimes   frequently   always

15. I would make better choices if I talked to my adult child beforehand.
    never   sometimes   frequently   always

16. My adult child wants me to seek his or her input more frequently.
    never   sometimes   frequently   always

17. My adult child wants me to seek his or her input less frequently.
    never   sometimes   frequently   always

18. When I think about my son or daughter's role in my life, he or she is most like a:
    son or daughter   friend   parent

LINDA M. HERMAN © 2013

These surveys have no right or wrong answers. They are included here to encourage your reflection about how you and your adult child relate to one another. At one time or another, most parents wish for a new level of contact with their children. They may envy the mother who goes to lunch with her daughter weekly to share gossip, or the mother whose independent daughter keeps her problems to herself. What kind of relationships do you have with your adult child? Are you satisfied? Would you want to change anything about the way you and your child connect?

- - - - - - - - - - - -

Is Your Child's Behavior a Problem?

Sometimes parents are worried about an adult child's behavior, but unsure of what, if anything, to do. Before taking any action it is important to determine whether a problem actually exists. The simple rule I use is this: *If a behavior interferes with someone's work or play, then there is a problem.* Once we've determined a problem behavior does exist, we can go further and identify the person who "owns" it. For example, if a mother is troubled by her adult son's behavior but the son is content with his actions, then the problem belongs to the mother. She may desperately wish for him to change, but needs to accept that he may not. The important point is that the meaning the behavior holds to the parent is often more telling than the behavior itself. Below are some questions intended to help bring clarity to your concerns.

PART ONE: DOES YOUR CHILD HAVE
A REAL OR PERCEIVED BEHAVIOR PROBLEM?

1. What is your child doing that you do not like?

2. How do you think this behavior is a problem for him or her?

3. Does he or she even acknowledge it as a problem?

4. Does it impact his or her ability to function at work, or even get a job? (For high school and college students, school may be appropriately considered their job.)

5. How does it impact his or her life away from work?

6. Have his or her leisure activities changed?

7. What about the impact upon those around him or her (e.g. wife, girlfriend, child, you or other parents)?

8. Is he or she breaking the law? If so, then certainly it is a problem for the legal system.

PART TWO
HOW DOES THE PROBLEM AFFECT YOUR LIFE?

Often the behavior problems we perceive in our adult children are not problems for them as much as they are problems for us. The following questions will help you assess how the perception of a problem may affect your life and work. Your answers to these questions can be helpful to talk through with other parents, as well as your friends, spouse, or therapist.

1. How does the behavior impact you?

2. Are you being affected at your job?

    a. Can you concentrate as well as usual?

    b. Are you missing work time because of the behavior?

    c. Has your performance at work deteriorated because of either time spent away from work or difficulty performing your usual tasks?

3. What about your time away from work?

    a. Have you withdrawn from others to avoid talking about your child?

    b. Are your relationships with other family members negatively affected?

    c. Have you changed your routine significantly?

    d. Have you given up your hobbies or interests?

e. Are your finances impacted by your child's actions?

f. What happens to you when you even think about your child's behavior?

PART THREE
HOW DOES THE BEHAVIOR AFFECT YOUR RELATIONSHIP?

Just as important as identifying a problem behavior is understanding what it means to you, as your child's parent. Here are a few additional questions:

1. What does this behavior mean to you?

2. What do you believe the behavior says about you as a parent?

3. What does it say about your child?

4. What does it say about your relationship with your child?

Your answers to these questions will give you vital clues as to the nature of the problem, who owns it, and how to approach working toward a solution. You may decide that you can directly address the issues with your adult child by taking action to change his or her behavior. Or, your challenge may be to accept a situation that you cannot control or influence, in which case you have to work to keep yourself healthy. Talking with a counselor or friend may help you put any situation in perspective.

Worksheets

PERSONAL COPING SKILLS
FOR PARENTS OF ADULT CHILDREN

1. Name a situation with your adult child or children that has recently caused you stress.

2. Identify who owns the problem. What part, if any, is yours and what part belongs to your adult child?

    a. Are you upset about something that is your adult child's issue?

    b. How might you be contributing to the problem?

3. Develop an action plan.

    a. What can you do to help your adult child in the situation? Does your child want to help? Talk to him or her to find out. List three specific actions you plan to take in the next month.

    b. Maybe the situation is beyond your control. Or perhaps your child does not want or need your involvement. That doesn't mean you're no longer upset. What can you do to keep yourself safe and healthy?

        i. Identify any direct actions you can take to improve your health and safety.

        ii. What can you do to help yourself emotionally?

iii.   What can you do to help yourself spiritually?

iv.   What can you do to help yourself physically?

4. Identify some of the blessings in your life. Regardless of the gravity of you situation, look for something for which you are grateful. This does not diminish the importance of your concerns, but reminds you that you also find pleasure in your life.

LINDA M. HERMAN © 2013

PERSONAL PLANNING FOR YOUNG ADULTS

1. Describe yourself

    a.   What are some of your strengths?

    b.   What are some of your challenges or difficulties?

    c.   What are your interests? What do you like to do?

    d.   What would you like your life to look like in __ year(s)?

    e.   What would be the "nightmare vision" of your life in __ year(s)?

    f.   What kind of setting can you see yourself working in (e.g., office, outdoors, dressy, casual)?

    g.   Taking into account what you wrote above, what would be a reasonable goal(s) to set for yourself (e.g., job, apartment)?

2. What do I need in order to get to my goal? That is, what are some short-term goals or objectives I have to master first (e.g., seeking job training, preparing a resume, finding transportation, attending to medical needs or emotional issues)? List these below:

    Short-term Goals

    1. _____

    2. _____

    3. _____

    4. _____

3. For each short-term goal, list actions you can take. If your long-term goal is to get a job, then a short-term goal might be to put together a resume. What steps must you take to achieve this? These might include conducting online research about writing resumes, making a list of your skills and job experiences, or meeting with someone who is skilled at preparing resumes.

Short-term Goal   Actions to Take   Timeline

1. _____

2. _____

3. _____

4. _____

Notes

Chapter Two

1. Jean M. Twenge, et al., "Birth cohort increases in psychopathology among young Americans, 1938–2007: A cross-temporal meta-analysis of the MMPI," *Clinical Psychology Review* 30 (2010): 145-54; Shirley Wang,"Is Happiness Overrated?" *Wall Street Journal*, March 15, 2011.
2. Jean Illsley Clark, Connie Dawson, and David Bredehoft, *How Much Is Enough?* (New York: Marlowe and Company, 2004).

Chapter Four

1. J. H. Pryor, et al., "The American Freshman: National Norms for Fall 2009," Higher Education Research Institute, UCLA, 2009.
2. David T. Ellwood and Christopher Jencks, "The Spread of Single Parent Families in the United States since 1960," working paper RWP04-008, John F. Kennedy School of Government, Harvard University, June 2004.
3. Janis Abrahms Spring, *After the Affair* (New York: Harper Collins, 1996), 169.
4. Roy F. Baumeister, et al. "Does High Self-Esteem Cause Better Performance, Interpersonal Success, Happiness, or Healthier Lifestyles?" *Psychological Science in the Public Interest* 4, no. 1 (2003): 1-39; and "Exploding the Self-Esteem Myth," *Scientific American*, January 2005: 84-91.
5. Jean M. Twenge and Keith Campbell, *The Narcissism Epidemic: Living in the Age of Entitlement* (New York: The Free Press, 2009), 290-291.
6. Ibid, 290.
7. Pauline Rose Clance and Suzanne Imes, "The Imposter Phenomenon in High-Achieving Women: Dynamics and Therapeutic Intervention," *Psychotherapy Theory, Research and Practice* 15, no. 3 (1978).

Chapter Five

1. Leo Kanner, "Frosted Children," *Time Magazine*, April 26, 1948.
2. Bruno Bettelheim, *The Empty Fortress: Infantile Autism and the Birth of the Self* (New York: Simon and Schuster, 1967).
3. Andrew Weil, *Spontaneous Healing* (New York: Random House, 1995).
4. June P. Tangey and Ronda L. Dearing, *Shame and Guilt* (New York: Guilford Press, 2002).
5. Ruth Benedict, *The Chrysanthemum and the Sword* (New York: Houghton-Mifflin, 1946; First Mariners Books, 2005), 222. Citations are to First Mariners edition.
6. Albert Ellis, *Overcoming Destructive Beliefs, Feelings, and Behaviors: New Directions for Rational Emotive Behavior Therapy* (Amherst: Prometheus Books, 2001); Aaron Beck, *Cognitive Therapy and the Emotional Disorders* (Madison, Connecticut: International Universities Press, 1976); David Burns, *Feeling Good: The New Mood Therapy* (New York: Avon Books, 1999).
7. Daniel G. Amen, *Change Your Brain, Change Your Life* (New York: Three Rivers Press, 1998).

Chapter Six

1. Margaret Mahler, F. Pine, and A. Bergman, *The Psychological Birth of the Human Infant*, (New York: Basic Books, 1973).
2. Louise Bates Ames and Frances L. Ilg, *Your Two-Year-Old: Terrible or Tender* (New York: Delacorte Press, 1980); and *Your Three-Year-Old: Friend or Enemy* (New York: Delacorte Press, 1980).
3. Anthony E. Wolf, *Get Out of My Life, But First Could You Drive Me and Cheryl to the Mall?* (New York: Farrar Straus Giroux, 2002).
4. Psychological and Counseling Center, Vanderbilt University, www.vanderbilt.edu/pcc/student-services/self-exploration-questions (accessed January 26, 2012).

Chapter Seven

1. Anne Ford, *On Their Own: Creating an Independent future for Your Adult Child with Learning Disabilities and ADHD*, (New York: Newmarket Press, 2007).

Chapter Eleven

1. US Department of Commerce, Economics and Statistics Administration, *Living Arrangements of Children: 2004* (Washington, DC: US Census Bureau, February, 2008).

2. Rudolph Dreikurs and Vicki Soltz, *Children: The Challenge* (New York: Penguin Books, 1990).

Chapter Twelve

1. American Psychiatric Association, "Healthy Minds. Healthy Lives," http://healthyminds.org/More-Info-For/GayLesbianBisexuals.aspxHealthyMinds.org.
2. American Psychiatric Association, "Therapies Focused on Attempts to 'Change Sexual Orientation' (Reparative or Conversion Therapies)" position statement, 200001a, http://www.psych.org/Departments/EDU/Library/APAOfficialDocumentsandRelated/PositionStatements/200001a.aspx (accessed February 24, 2012).

Chapter Thirteen

1. Alvin Goldman, *Ethics* (Chicago: University of Chicago Press, 1993), 103, 337-360.
2. Pinchas Noy, "The Three Components of Empathy: Normal and Pathological Development," in *Empathy*, eds. J. Lichtenberg; M. Bornstein and D. Silver, (Hillsdale, New Jersey: The Analytic Press, 1984), 167-199.
3. Judith Orloff, *Emotional Freedom: Liberate Yourself From Negative Emotions and Transform Your Life* (New York: Harmony Books, 2009), 106-107.
4. Elaine N. Aron, *The Highly Sensitive Person*, (New York: Broadway Books, 1996).
5. Ibid., 10-11.
6. Shelley Taylor, et al.," Biobehavioral Responses to Stress in Females: Tend-and-Befriend, Not Fight-or-Flight," *Psychological Review*, 107, no. 3 (2000): 411-29.

Chapter Fourteen

1. Compassionate Friends, "When a Child Dies: A Survey of Bereaved Parents Conducted by NFO Research on Behalf of The Compassionate Friends," June 1999 -http://www.compassionatefriends.org/pdf/When_a_Child_Dies_-_1999_Survey.pdf (accessed February 24, 2012).
2. Ibid.
3. Ibid.
4. Compassionate Friends, "When a Child Dies: A Survey of Bereaved Parents Conducted by Directions Research for The Compassionate Friends," October 2006 – http://www.compassionatefriends.org/pdf/When_a_Child_Dies-2006_Final.pdf (accessed February 24, 2012).
5. Jeanne Webster Blank, *The Death of an Adult Child* (Amityville, New York: Baywood Publishing Company, 1998).

6. Elisabeth Kübler-Ross, *On Death and Dying* (New York: Scribner, 2005).

7. Elizabeth Kübler-Ross and David Kessler, *On Grief and Grieving: Finding the Meaning of Grief Through the Five Stages of Loss*, (New York: Scribner, 2005).

8. See note 5.

9. See note 5; 24.

10. Mothers of Incarcerated Sons Society (M.I.S.S.), http://www.mothersofin-mates.org (accessed February 15, 2012).

11. PrisonTalk Online, http://www.prisontalk.com (accessed February 15, 2012).

12. See note 7; 2-3.

Chapter Fifteen

1. Fred Luskin, *Forgive for Good* (San Francisco: Harper Collins, 2002); Robert Enright, *Forgiveness is a Choice* (Washington, DC: The American Psychological Association, 2001).

2. See note 1, Luskin; 68-69.

3. See note 1, Enright; 31.

4. See note 1, Luskin; 51.

5. See note 1, Luskin; 87.

6. Lewis B. Smedes, *The Art of Forgiving* (New York: Random House, 1996), 58.

7. Ibid., 178.

8. Susan Forward, *Toxic Parents: Overcoming Their Hurtful Legacy and Reclaiming Your Life* (New York: Bantam Books, 1989), 191.

9. See note 1, Luskin; 79.

Chapter Sixteen

1. David Shenk, *The Genius in All of Us* (New York: Doubleday, 2010), 18.

2. Ibid., 27.

3. Carol Dweck and Claudia Mueller, "Praise for Intelligence Can Undermine Children's Motivation and Performance," *Journal of Personality and Social Psychology*, 75, no. 1 (1998): 33-52; Lisa Blackwell, Kali Trzesniewski, and Carol Dweck, "Implicit Theories of Intelligence Predict Achievement Across an Adolescent Transition: A Longitudinal Study and an Intervention," *Child Development*, 78 no. 1 (2007): 246-63.

4. Ibid., Dweck and Mueller.

5. Ibid., Dweck and Mueller.

6. Ibid., Dweck and Mueller.

7. See note 1; 80.

8. See note 1; 27.

9. Thomas J. Stanley and William D. Danko, *The Millionaire Next Door: The Surprising Secrets of America's Wealthy* (New York: Simon and Shuster, 1996), 23.

10. Ibid., 25.

11. Joseph A. Califano Jr., "What Was Really Great About the Great Society," *The Washington Monthly Online*, October 1999, http://www.washington-monthly.com (accessed Feb. 15, 2012).

12. Robin Dion et al., "Helping Unwed Parents Build Strong and Healthy Marriages: A Conceptual Framework for Interventions," (Washington, DC: US Department of Health and Human Services, January 2003).

13. See note 9; 142.

14. See note 9 above; 149.

15. Malcolm S. Knowles, Elwood F. Holton, and Richard A. Swanson, *The Adult Learner:The Definitive Classic in Adult Education and Human Resource Development,* 6th edition (Oxford: Butterworth-Heinemann, 2005).

Chapter Seventeen

1. "The Return of the Multi-Generational Family Household," Pew Research Center, Washington, DC, March 18, 2010, http://www.pewsocialtrends.org/2010/03/18/the-return-of-the-multi-generational-family-household/.

2. Gretchen Livingston and D'Vera Cohn, "The New Demography of American Motherhood," Pew Research Center, Washington, DC, May 6, 2010, revised August 19, 2010, http://pewresearch.org/pubs/1586/changing-demographic-characteristics-american-mothers.

3. Sarah Fenwick, "Greece Q2 Jobless Rate Rises to 16.3 percent q/q," *Cyprus News Report*, http://www.cyprusnewsreport.com/?q=node/4634.

4. "Q &A: Greece's Economic Woes," *BBC News*, May 2, 2010, http://news.bbc.co.uk/2/mobile/business/8508136.stm.

5. "EU piles pressure on Italy in crisis talks," *Sydney Morning Herald*, October 24, 2011, http://www.smh.com.au/business/world-business/eu-piles-pressure-on-italy-in-crisis-talks-20111024-1meyt.html.

6. "KIPPERS are eating up their parents' retirement savings," *The Birmingham Post*, November 17, 2003, http://www.highbeam.com/doc/1G1-110210374.html.

7. Kumiko Nemoto, "Postponed Marriage: Exploring Women's Views of Matrimony and Work in Japan" *Gender and Society*, 22, no. 2 (2008): 219-37.

8. Tamaki Saito, "Trend of 'big baby adult children living with parents goes global,'" *Mainichi Daily News*, March 30, 2010.

Chapter Nineteen

1. Patricia Sprinkle, *Women Who Do Too Much* (Grand Rapids: Zondervan, 1992); Robin Norwood, *Women Who Love Too Much*, (New York: Simon and Schuster, 2008).

Index